DRAWING
AS A MEANS TO ARCHITECTURE

William Kirby Lockard

ϕ PEPPER PUBLISHING

Copyright © 1977
WILLIAM KIRBY LOCKARD

Revised Edition, January 1977
Library of Congress number 76-47137
ISBN 0-914468-04-9

Printed in the United States of America

Published by
PEPPER PUBLISHING
2901 East Mabel Street
Tucson, Arizona 85716

Available in Spanish from
Editorial Trillas, S.A.
Av. 5 de Mayo 43-105
Apartado Postal 10534
Mexico 1, D.F.

NOTES ON THE REVISED EDITION

In architecture or education the opportunity to revise your previous work is rare indeed. Awkward buildings and inept teaching persist, at least in the conscience of the designer or the teacher long beyond the time to do anything about them. Books, however, can occasionally be revised, and I welcome the opportunity to make a few additions and one correction to a publication which is now almost ten years old.

Almost all the revisions are the result of an effort to reduce the cost of the book in the face of tremendous increases in the cost of paper, printing and binding over the last nine years. The reduction in size, the change to a standard binding and the collection of the colored and tissue pages into even eight-page signatures hopefully gain more in the price reduction they allow than they lose in the few relationships in the original edition which had to be foresaken.

The major error which this edition corrects is the use of vanishing points for diagonals in the perspective method rather than the shortcut approximations advocated in the first edition. I have found that the location and use of the vanishing points for diagonals is perhaps even quicker and deepens the student's understanding of perspective in general.

The additions to the book are all the results of taking advantage of the adjustments necessary to reorganize the book into even eight-page signatures. This reshuffling allowed me to add the exterior and night perspectives under DIAZO PROCESS PRINTS; a brief method of shadow-casting in perspective under LIGHT; and a new tracing paper signature under EFFICIENCY AND WISDOM IN DRAWING, which introduces the idea of considering drawing as an investment hierarchy. I also suggest some shortcuts to tonal interest when drawing on tracing paper and propose that much of drawing is learned as perceptual tapes or templates.

I believe the main concepts of the book remain as valid as they were when I wrote them, and I'm not sure I could say them any more strongly or clearly than I did a decade ago. Drawing is still a designer's most valuable and learnable skill; and our professional schools are probably doing even less today to demythologize drawing ability or teach it with the patience, clarity and commitment it deserves.

William Kirby Lockard
Tucson   1977

CONTENTS

ACKNOWLEDGMENTS

It may seem presumptuous in so short a book to take a page to acknowledge sources of help and encouragement, but I think it would be much more presumptuous of me to leave you with the impression that this work was conceived and delivered unaided.

For me, one of the valued characteristics of drawing is the way it and the values that nurture it are passed from one hand and mind to another hand and mind. This source for me was my mother, Zella Mangold Lockard, and my grandmother, Effie Rich Mangold, who took the time and expended the patience to begin to teach me to draw.

My architect employers while I served as an architect-in-training, Emerson Scholer, Nicholas Sakellar, Santry Fuller, Bernard Friedman, and Fred Jobusch, were patient enough, and valued drawing enough, to pay me for what must have seemed endless hours spent developing much of the thought and technique which this book contains.

I am also grateful to Dean Sidney Little and my fellow teachers at the University of Arizona for their consistent encouragement. The University of Arizona Alumni Association was generous in a grant to help publish the pilot edition. I am fairly sure that students make a teacher rather than the reverse. I am very sure that my students have made, or shaped, much of the content of this book, and I appreciate their contribution.

Mrs. Catherine Bell proofread my first attempts at writing and I am grateful for her criticism as I am for that of Ellery Green, who read, and helped me improve, the section "Drawings As Communications."

William Kirby Lockard

Books on drawing often begin with a chapter on how the drawing instrument should be held. Not wishing to break with tradition I say only:

If you would learn to draw
Hold the instrument often
and hold it with your head.

INTRODUCTION

I have two goals in writing this book. The simpler one is to develop a workbook to help teach drawing to beginning architectural students. The more difficult task I would attempt is that of making a plea for drawing as a means to architecture, and a defense of drawing as a mental rather than a physical discipline.

Skill in architectural drawing is often dismissed as a happy gift of co-ordination of hand and eye, incapable or unworthy of being learned or taught, and having little to do with the intellectual design process. Architects who have taken the trouble to learn to draw well may even find the accomplishment sometimes casts doubt on their design ability. This stigma is strong enough to give me misgivings about authoring a book about drawing lest I be classified as a delineator and therefore categorically *not* a designer. This attitude has always offended me because I am sure that drawing can and should be learned and taught. Drawing is as important to the design process as any other ability. I am sure, also, that drawing demands more mind than hand and in fact *is* design.

Yet with all its importance, drawing must never become the end. It is still only a means to architecture. Accepting drawing as an end can be quite satisfying and most books on architectural drawing are written by "drawing as an end" people. The fallacy is that architectural drawing must be "means" drawing

to have any validity. "Artists' conceptions" and all sketches made by delineators not concerned with the detailing, construction and budget are irresponsible and invalid, precisely because the drawing becomes the end, and not the means. It is as if there were people who made "rough manuscripts" for writers or composers.

The architect's primary reason for learning to draw is to possess a tool with which he can test his first conceptual ideas, discard, refine them, and finally, but only secondarily, present them to others.

Architects have too long used as their models for drawing the labored presentations of professional architectural renderers. This type of rendering is altogether frustrating to the architectural student and the practitioner alike, since the student feels that he will never have the skill and the practitioner knows that he will never have the time.

I have written as nearly as I have been able the determinants or rationalizations for the way I draw. These may not all be true for you, but they may be useful to indicate that strong drawing needs a certain philosophy, or point of view, always changing, but always present. I do not propose this point of view dogmatically for I believe in open-ended systems and the responsibility for continually extending and restructuring them in drawing. When you read this, my ideas about drawing hopefully will have altered somewhat and the main value of this book should be to persuade you to begin the continual process of formation and change that any serious endeavor deserves.

The workbook form seems appropriate, since the publication grows out of a need for a text at the University of Arizona and the hope that the book will spend more time at the drawing board than on the shelf. I hope you will draw in the book, trace parts of it if that will help you learn, and that you will save additional sketching references in the form of clippings in a file or other convenient place.

Consistent with the purposes stated, I have limited the techniques to those which can be used in normal architectural practice — using minimal equipment but taking advantage of available reproduction techniques.

The drawings in this book are almost all line drawings. Line drawings are less expensive to reproduce, but more important, line is the most efficient way to draw. It requires only one simple tool, a pen or pencil of any kind, and describes forms and spaces with an absolute minimum of time and effort. Line is the technique required for working drawings in architectural practice, and it seems reasonable that, given a limited amount of time, a designer would be wise to concentrate on the development of a single graphic technique.

Most of the drawings were done with a set of three "Rapidograph" pens—3, 1 and 00. I would have preferred to make all the drawings like the two quick sketches in the overlay series (pages 82 and 84), which were drawn with fountain pen, Prismacolor pencils, and felt-tip markers on buff tracing paper. This technique is the most effective I have found in relation to the time it takes. Reproducing such sketches is quite complicated and very expensive, however, so most of the drawings are in the tighter *line* technique.

All the drawings are reproduced at the same size they were drawn except for a few small sketches and the plan, section, elevation, which were reduced from 24″ x 36″ sheets. I believe full-size examples are important since most architectural drawings are greatly reduced for publication, and the reduction, while flattering to the drawing, makes any study of the drawing technique very difficult. With the exception of the two working drawings, all drawings are freehand: most of them are overlays over drafted or freehand frameworks.

If you believe that design is important and that it is a cognitive process which is more or less continuous, then pare your design equipment down to your mind, a pen, and any piece of paper. Learn to design sketch with the same instrument you normally carry. I use a one-dollar "Sheaffer" cartridge pen. The designer is crippled if he depends on a room full of equipment. With a little training of your hand you can learn to do all the drawings necessary to conceive and study an architectural design without going near a drafting room and its equipment. This ability allows you to design anywhere, anytime.

There are other reasons for learning to draw freehand. One is a matter of the dignity of the craft of drawing. The human hand is capable of fantastic skill, and architects should be responsible for valuing that potential skill in drawing as well as in carpentry or masonry.

The last reason is a very practical one. Although modern architects have almost succeeded in reducing all architecture to the orthogonal grid, architectural entourage cannot be reduced to drafting. Trees, figures, and cars will always require freehand delineation and will conflict in line character with a drafted building. So real consistency in architectural drawing can be achieved only by drawing everything with the same freehand line.

Without presenting any further argument for an architect's learning to draw, I would insist that what we design and build is still *absolutely* limited to what we can draw. This limitation will apply as long as we rely on drawings to present our ideas to clients and contractors. One of the real reasons why we no longer ornament like Sullivan is that we can't draw like Sullivan. Perhaps the greatest appeal the curtain wall has for the modern architect is that it can be drawn by an idiot or a machine, and should be, being beneath the dignity of the attention of man's hand.

I have found it meaningful to compare the limitations drawing imposes on design to the similar limitations the available construction technology imposes. The available construction technology is, or should be, as strong a determinant and as much a part of the context into which the building is to be built as the site, the climate, and the contemporary esthetic. While an architect is always responsible to design buildings which will challenge and improve the existing technology, he must know the technology's limitations and respect them if his designs are to be successfully constructed.

In school the final product, instead of being a building, is a set of presentation drawings. The technology available to the student (his drawing ability) should be a design determinant from the beginning of the design process if the final product is to be successful. Between presentations he should strive to improve this drawing ability, but he must respect its limitations in designing and "building" a presentation.

In talking about drawing, I have inevitably included many of my ideas about architecture since it is, for me, impossible to separate the two. I have also tried to show how the two are interrelated and have a marked effect on one another. Many of contemporary architecture's weaknesses, I believe, can be traced to the weaknesses of contemporary architectural drawing.

William Kirby Lockard

Tucson   1967

9

THE DRAWINGS

Centuries of architectural practice have established four drawings with which to design, communicate, and construct buildings. They are *plan*, *elevation*, *section*, and *perspective*. They are generally, and unfortunately, placed in that order of importance, using as a measure the amount of time, and especially design time, spent with each drawing.

I believe the order might better be *perspective*, *plan/section*, and *elevation*, although the order should never become rigid. Some concepts exist most strongly in section, some in plan, some in elevation, but they all must exist in perspective. For the post-construction life of a building, which is certainly most of its life, and can be said to be its only significant life, the experience of the building is *totally* perspective. We speak of "space" and "spatial relations" and "spatial sequences" *ad nauseam*, yet we often ignore the only drawing which really shows the third dimension. And when it is used we waste it by drawing buildings as objects rather than as spaces.

"Yes," you say, "but the other drawings *are* spatial. Read the writings of those, mostly painters, who have so influenced the basic design courses for architects. Experience the spatial dynamics and tensions on the two-dimensional surface." Wonderful, but how can this be news to architects? We own the *real* third dimension and always have. Manipulation on a two-dimensional surface is "flatland" and not worth the vast amounts of time we lavish on plan studies, particularly. And here I continue to speak relatively, as I suggest well over fifty per cent of design effort is normally expended on plan.

You may say that this is because man moves on this plane and again quote me the basic design literature. And I will answer that I suspect that this preoccupation with plan is by default, because it is easier. It is a heritage from the surveyor, the realtor, and the zoning ordinance, or perhaps the relative position of plans on drawing boards. We accept this flatland because it is expedient and because *we never learned how to draw perspectives.*

Perhaps more important than the relative importance of the four drawings is their inadequacy today for design, for communication and, perhaps, for construction. I suspect that this inadequacy of graphic means can be laid, if we are honest, to expediency, not to say laziness. At a time when communications are becoming increasingly sophisticated, architects persist in the monosyllabic vocabulary of plan, section, and elevation. Any drawings beyond these are viewed as suspect and superfluous "eyewash." A request for such a drawing by a principal in an architectural firm is rare and normally put forth with the caution, "Now don't spend too much time on this."

An even more shameful circumstance is that such a drawing is an after-the-fact presentation drawing, and so of no value in design. And often there is no one in an office who can depend ably produce such a drawing and it is farmed out to a professional renderer. And so, in a profession concerned with esthetics, we have surrendered the esthetics of our architectural practice to Madison Avenue.

In the last part of this section I would like to suggest what some new graphic means might be. I am sure that there are many actually in use today. I have asked fifth-year students to use experimental design graphics in studying and presenting their terminal projects. I have also used similar graphics in my own practice. In both cases I have often experienced more success with unconventional graphics as study and communicative devices than with the conventional orthographic projections.

The drawings necessary to construct a building have always been plan, section, and elevation at various scales. These the architect is obligated to produce in order to *build* a building. But I am not persuaded they are the only, or even the best, graphic means to the *design* of a building. I can find no logic to prove that the instrument for construction should be the same as that for design. This would reduce to *design = construction*, and I do not believe this is true.

PERSPECTIVE

Perspective is the most natural way of drawing space, since it is how we see space; yet in architectural education the habit of avoiding drawing perspectives begins early. The architectural professor begins with plan, section, and elevation, which are architectural abstractions and the secret language of the profession. The student grasps the simplicity of these drawings and appreciates the fact that they can be drafted. Later, when he is taught the elaborate method of perspective construction, he has been brainwashed by the T-square and triangle and assumes that since there *is* an exact way of constructing a perspective, and architecture *seems* to be a technical discipline, the *only* way to draw three-dimensional space is by laborious projection.

This attitude toward perspective is compounded by the procedure of requiring a plan, then a section, then elevations (hopefully the section comes before the elevations), and then, on the final presentation, *the* perspective.

This is nonsense. The experience of a building is an infinite number of perspectives; most of them interior. Yet, very possibly, not one was used in studying the design, and when the final perspective is drawn, the building is ugly. To me this seems perfectly reasonable. If a perspective was not used in studying the design, why should the building be beautiful in perspective? When the student is disappointed in this way, he naturally feels frustrated and blames his ugly building on the

11

fact that he just can't draw perspectives. His professor has encouraged the design, the student has been excited about it, yet his crowning picture is ugly. The experience is shattering and he avoids perspectives from that time on. He even rationalizes them to a position of no importance.

Experienced architects can visualize three-dimensional space from plan and section, and these drawings are valid, helpful tools in studying a building, but I am sure that, drawing for drawing, they cannot compare with perspectives for depicting the experience of a building. Especially for the beginning student and the layman client, the perspective is as close to the reality of a building as drawing can get.

The first and all the successive traumatic grapplings of the architectural student with perspective justify its being taught as a primary architectural drawing. For that reason I deal with it first in this book.

I wish to make clear that I value the method which follows not because of its accuracy or its solid basis in optical science, but because its study-value/effort ratio is good enough to make it a drawing method which can be used in designing a building.

The other methods are certainly more accurate but they are subject to certain very arbitrary limitations, and so complex that they are not worth using as study drawings. The fact that the normal methods are rarely used in architectural design is enough to question their validity and at least consider methods such as that which follows.

Architectural Space

I believe that the manner in which the architectural profession presents its building designs is both a sign of, and perhaps a contributor to, the way we think of architecture, to our great shame.

Architects draw perspectives of buildings as objects to be viewed from without — across the street, from a great height or some special inhuman position from which the viewer can grasp the entire building complex in one glorious full-color view. I don't believe this type of drawing has anything to do with architecture. It is merely a device of the news media which assume that the reality of a building can be shown in one aerial photograph.

Architectural space is enclosed space; defined space, interior space. We present buildings as if they were to be walked around and viewed from afar, but never entered. We picture them, or allow professional renderers to picture them, as self-sufficient entities, having no relation to neighboring buildings or other aspects of their real environment.

This manner of presentation is symptomatic of the ills of modern architecture. From three hundred yards we can see all there is to see, in one instant. There is no further interest, nor the promise of any: no interesting spaces around or behind or within the building. It is all over in a glance. We think of our buildings as objects, ignoring the possibility of using them to shape exterior space. Thus, for me, the best way to draw architectural space is from within the space. In drawing space from within, the two standard methods give us two very strange views of a space. A two-point perspective will show only two enclosing walls of the space and appear to the viewer as if he had been sent to stand in the corner. There is very little sense of either horizontal dimension of the space.

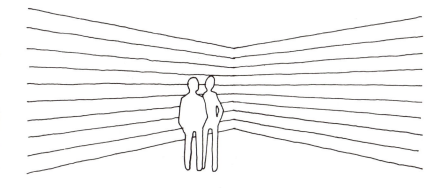

The one-point perspective is also objectionable. It does show three enclosing walls and one of the horizontal dimensions of the space, but it is so deadly static that it glues the viewer on axis like a bride coming down the aisle.

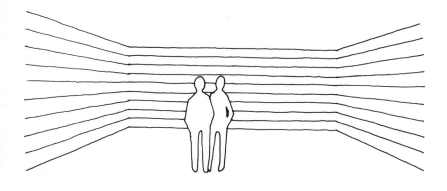

Identity

The primary goal in perspective drawing is the establishment of the identity of the viewer in space. Clients invariably say, "Let's see. Where are we looking from?" I have found two ways of establishing the relation of the viewer to a perspective. The first is to take the perspective eyeball-high from a level which is common to other people, not halfway up a stair or from a tree across the road. This is easily established by drawing the horizon line and several figures of different sizes with the horizon running through their heads. This establishes two horizontal planes; the plane on which we are standing and the "eyeball" plane five feet high. Any figure standing on the same plane will have his eyes at the same level. This common eye level goes a long way toward establishing identity since the viewer is obviously standing on the same level with these other people. *The drawing of the horizon and several figures should always be the first step in drawing a perspective.*

The other means of relating the viewer to the space of the perspective is partly psychological, partly expedient. I find that one-point perspectives are dull, since all the lines running across the drawing are parallel, a very unreal coincidence, at least the way I perceive space. The normal two-point perspective is strangely and stupidly limited by the size of the drawing board. This limitation leaves a great gap in between, in which, for me, lie the perspectives closest to reality. Let us assume a two-point perspective — one vanishing point a great distance to one side and the other within our picture.

We can set this up freehand by adding to the horizon a series of tapering lines fanning out in one direction or the other. It is important that the tapering be very slight, but proportionately greater as the lines progress up and down from the horizon.

Now assume another vanishing point within the picture near the wide end of the tapered lines and draw a bordering plane just outside that vanishing point. At this point the spatial structuring begins to be established. We have established a vanishing point farther away than we could possibly reach for projection and our space has the vitality of being off the deadly, static processional axis of one-point perspectives. Also, we are psychologically more comfortable in the space, since we are not entirely in the open, exposed and friendless. We are near a wall and we perceive the space from the protection of our relation to the wall.

Spatial Structuring

The method of structuring space shown in the chart across page is simply a ten-foot cube version of the Euclidean concept of space, viewed in a particular way for the preceding reasons. The ten-foot cube is especially convenient since it is twice eye-level, and we are comfortable with a math base of ten and can easily interpolate a ten-foot cube into one-foot increments.

In sketching a perspective by this method, the structuring should follow this order. First, draw the horizon and some figures. Then draw two tapering lines equally spaced above and below the horizon. These will be zero elevation or ground level and a ten-foot height, the horizon assumed to be at five-foot eye-level. It is easy then to make this ten-foot high plane one of the walls, say the back wall, of the space you are drawing.

On this wall, which I have called the *measuring plane*, you can accurately mark off ten-foot squares. A diagonal of the square through the horizon will give you five feet and you can easily interpolate to feet or even fractions of feet. You may also reduce this wall to less than ten feet or raise it higher to correspond to the wall of the space you are drawing. Windows, doors, furniture, and brick coursing all may be laid out accurately on this measuring plane.

You should take as one of the sidewalls or limits of your space a sharply vanishing plane just to the wide side of the vanishing point (see "Identity," page 13). You may then measure along the measuring plane to the other side wall. This more splayed and directly viewed wall I have called the *depth-judgment* plane. All judgments of depth should be made along this plane and projected across the perspective to their correct location. If there is no such wall in the space you are drawing, it will still be necessary to draw such a plane on which to make depth judgments needed elsewhere in the perspective.

I use the word judgment because that is precisely what is involved. The first receding ten-foot square is entirely an estimation on the part of the designer as to what a ten-foot square would look like, vanishing at that angle. Once this judgment is made, other squares may be marked off rather accurately by projected diagonals as shown on the chart. You must always look at the overall space that develops and perhaps adjust your first depth judgment if it proves to be too deep or too shallow.

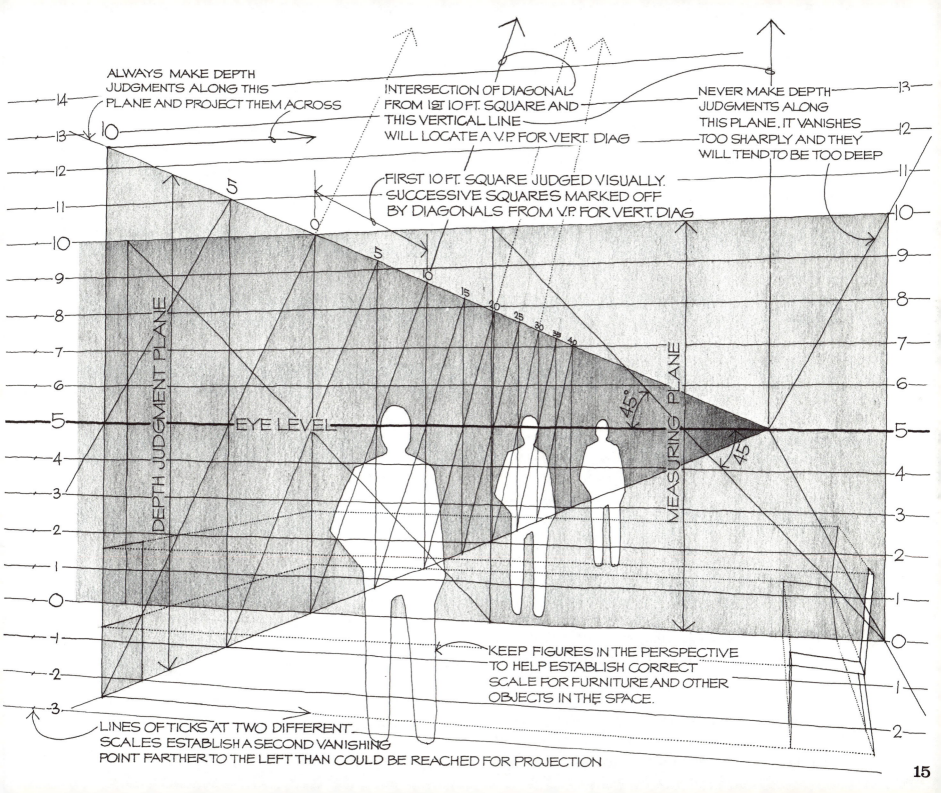

ALWAYS MAKE DEPTH JUDGMENTS ALONG THIS PLANE AND PROJECT THEM ACROSS

INTERSECTION OF DIAGONAL FROM 1ST 10 FT. SQUARE AND THIS VERTICAL LINE WILL LOCATE A V.P. FOR VERT. DIAG

NEVER MAKE DEPTH JUDGMENTS ALONG THIS PLANE. IT VANISHES TOO SHARPLY AND THEY WILL TEND TO BE TOO DEEP

FIRST 10 FT. SQUARE JUDGED VISUALLY. SUCCESSIVE SQUARES MARKED OFF BY DIAGONALS FROM V.P. FOR VERT. DIAG

DEPTH JUDGMENT PLANE

MEASURING PLANE

EYE LEVEL

45°

45°

KEEP FIGURES IN THE PERSPECTIVE TO HELP ESTABLISH CORRECT SCALE FOR FURNITURE AND OTHER OBJECTS IN THE SPACE.

LINES OF TICKS AT TWO DIFFERENT SCALES ESTABLISH A SECOND VANISHING POINT FARTHER TO THE LEFT THAN COULD BE REACHED FOR PROJECTION

That there is no set way of arriving at the correct depth in this method of drawing a perspective I have found to be a great advantage. It forces the designer to think in, and be responsible for, the third dimension. This third dimension is, for me, the *architectural* dimension more than any of the others, including time. The revelation of this third dimension is the reason for drawing a perspective, and I find a continued grappling with this dimension stimulating and desirable. Thus what could be considered arbitrary and an objectionable flaw in the method I find one of its strongest points.

In working with students I have found two harmful tendencies which you, by understanding them, may avoid. They are related to, and I think are partially attributable to, a preoccupation with plan view. The first tendency is to draw perspectives too deep. In a perspective of a room there is often great reluctance to foreshorten space and stack objects up so that they obscure the farthest objects. Students often insist on showing floor between each receding piece of furniture in a room. The result is that the space becomes ridiculously deep. I think one contributing factor may be that, having drawn a decent sofa, one hates to cover it up with a coffee table and then some chairs in the foreground.

The other tendency is to draw entirely too much foreground so that the viewer, by looking at the very bottom of the drawing, expects to see his own shoes. This tendency seems to be caused by a drive finally to get back to vertical plan view.

It also may be an attempt to establish the location or identity of the viewer, as I recommend doing in a different way. Drawing excessive foreground should be avoided because it distorts objectionably and because with the head held erect we do not clearly perceive the floor surface closer than eight or ten feet from where we sit and even further if we are standing.

The method put forward here is intended as a lightning-fast freehand study method. Rigid drawings are used only to show the method clearly. If you get into ticking off and ruling lines you would be better actually to project the perspective. It will be more accurate and take only a little longer.

Students often take this simple method as a great new all-purpose perspective method, and use it to attempt the construction of city-scapes, or complex interiors. This is like attempting to play Beethoven's *Ninth* on the harmonica. It is meant to be a simple, relatively accurate, study tool, *not a precise technique.*

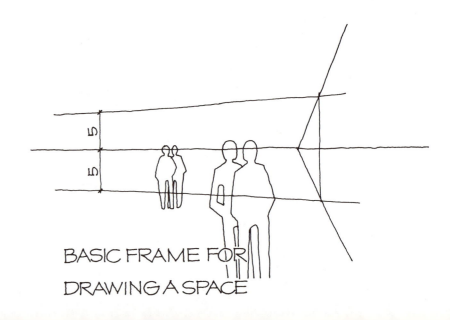

BASIC FRAME FOR
DRAWING A SPACE

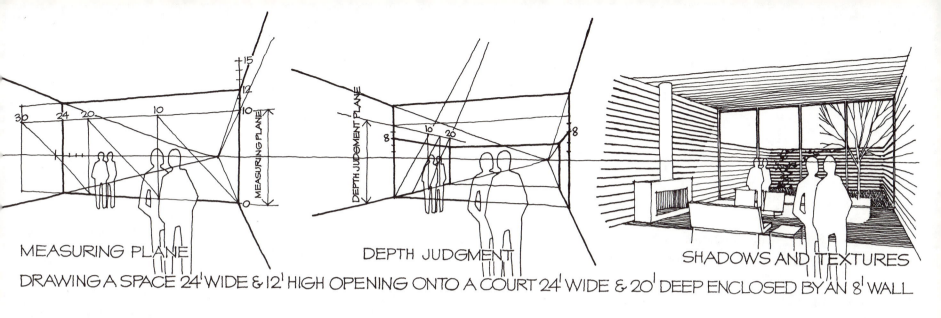

MEASURING PLANE   DEPTH JUDGMENT   SHADOWS AND TEXTURES

DRAWING A SPACE 24' WIDE & 12' HIGH OPENING ONTO A COURT 24' WIDE & 20' DEEP ENCLOSED BY AN 8' WALL

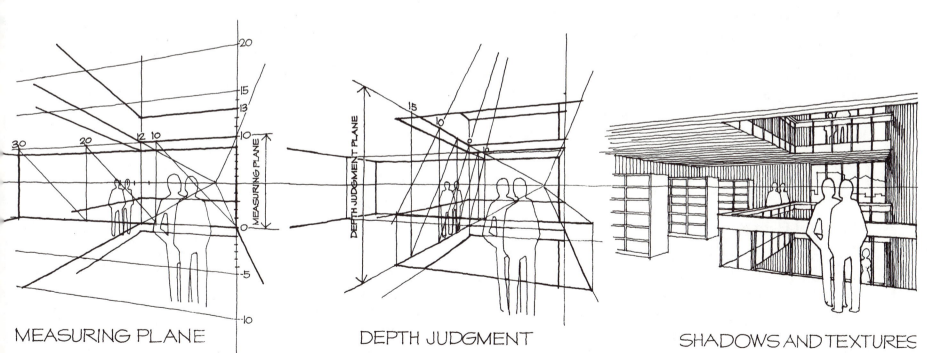

MEASURING PLANE   DEPTH JUDGMENT   SHADOWS AND TEXTURES

DRAWING A SPACE 30' WIDE & 9' HIGH CONNECTING VERTICALLY TO SIMILAR SPACES ABOVE & BELOW BY A 12' WIDE X 17' DEEP OPEN WELL SURROUNDED BY A 3' RAILING. WELL AT RIGHT SIDE OF THE SPACE

Plan, section, and elevation are the primary architectural drawings, although I hope you are now convinced that the perspective should be included as their equal. I can make no great contribution to what is generally known about these three drawings, but I think it is important to point out the difference between design drawings and construction drawings. Pages 20 through 23 show a comparison between design drawings and construction drawings in plan, section, and elevation. The construction drawings are taken from an actual set of working drawings. The design drawings are stripped of any entourage so that you may better see the drawings without benefit of cosmetics. It is possible to make a rather handsome drawing which shows nothing but architecture. To do this, you must make the most of line weight and shadows and concentrate on an economy of indication consistent with the elimination of entourage.

Plan and Section

The plan and section are actually both *sections*, one taken in the horizontal plane, the other in the vertical plane. Both drawings have very different purposes as design drawings and construction drawings. In construction drawings the plan and section cut through the construction to show in detail the way the building is to be put together. In design and presentation drawings their primary purpose is entirely different. That purpose is to cut through the building in order to show the positive and negative space: the space for human use being the positive space and all space within the surface of walls, above ceilings, and below floors being the negative space.

In construction drawing plan or section, the negative space is filled with details of beams, studs, ducts, hangers, etc. In a design plan or section, this negative space simply becomes so much "stuff" which is outside the human space, cannot be seen, and is therefore unimportant to the use or reality of the space. In the design plans and sections following it is simply poche'd as gray.

The envelope of negative space should be profiled with a very heavy line. This line which separates positive from negative space is the most important line in the drawing or in the building.

The Plan

The plan is a horizontal section and should be cut through the building at a height which goes through all wall openings, such as doors and windows. Show lines which occur above this section plane as dashed or dotted lines. Time permitting, the dotted line, as shown, is more sophisticated than the dashed line. One good way of indicating structure is with light center lines as shown.

Over-labeling is a very common mistake in the plan. If you draw a bathtub, water closet, and lavatory in a small room, it is hardly necessary to label it *bathroom*. What else could it be? Very simple indications of furniture or equipment in a room can identify its use more simply than writing a word within the room. The furniture or equipment has the added advantage of giving scale.

A simple building, such as the house shown here, often needs no labeling at all. If the plan is reasonable the use of the various spaces will be obvious.

The Section

Take care in choosing where you cut a section. In a construction section you should feel free to jog the section line so that it goes through as many different construction details as possible. Staggered sections, however, are not desirable in a design or presentation drawing. The jogs become confusing. Always take a design section in one continuous plane, where it can show the greatest number of relationships between interior spaces and look toward the most significant ends of the various spaces. I do not imply that one section is sufficient to study or describe a building. The designer must take many sections through his building in order to study the proportions and interrelationships of the interior spaces.

Always draw human figures and other scale-giving objects in design sections. They are necessary to give the correct scale to the spaces.

Always indicate a rather deep and extensive band of earth at the base of a section to show the building's relation to the site. In sheet composition with other drawings, the section, because of this dark band and the strong relation of the building to gravity, should always be placed at the bottom of the sheet.

The Elevation

Of the architectural drawings, the elevation, the least valuable for me, is, however, the best drawing to use in studying the proportions of the exterior of a building, its masses and openings. The weakness of elevation drawings is their lack of depth indication. This two-dimensional quality is the reason elevations cannot compare with perspectives for delineating the reality of a building.

The greatest difference between a construction elevation and a design elevation is the delineation and study of what light does on the form: the shades and shadows. Since shades and shadows help show depth in an elevation, the placement of the sun and its angle are very important. Search for a sun placement and angle which will best indicate the form of the building. Find this by sketching several different sun positions and choosing the best one.

Line weight and the idea of the spatial slice can also help indicate depth in elevation. The same rules apply as stated later in *line* drawing.

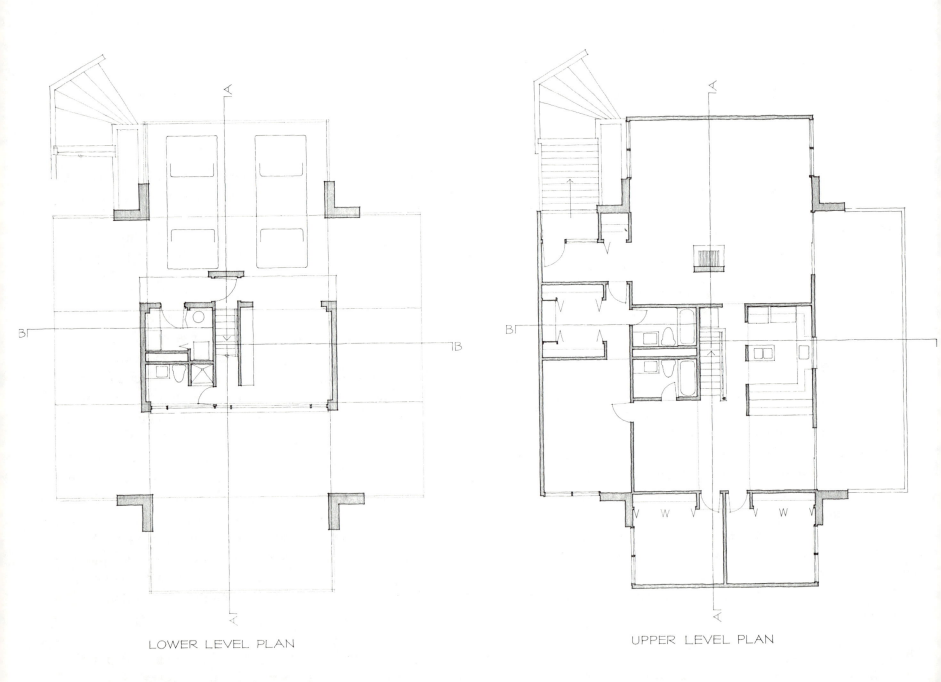

LOWER LEVEL PLAN

UPPER LEVEL PLAN

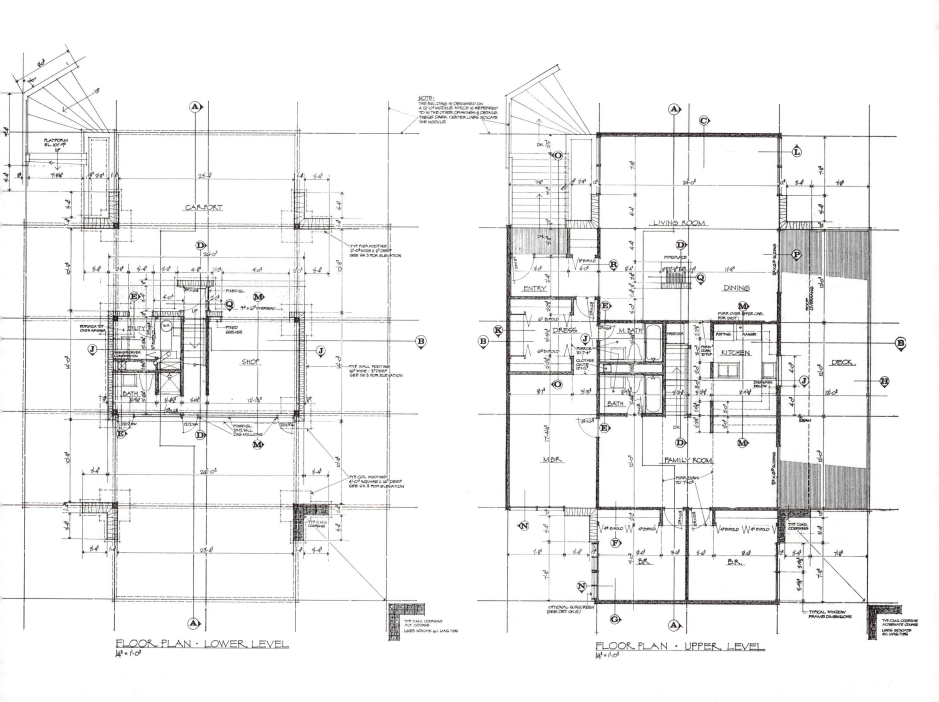

FLOOR PLAN · LOWER LEVEL
1/4" = 1'-0"

FLOOR PLAN · UPPER LEVEL
1/4" = 1'-0"

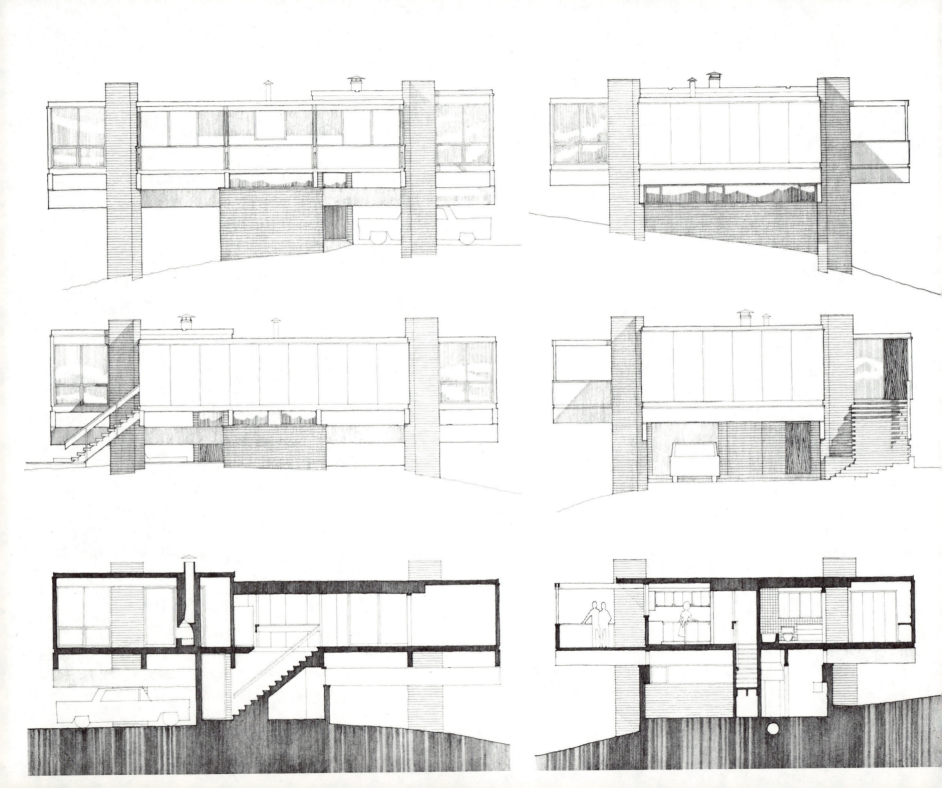

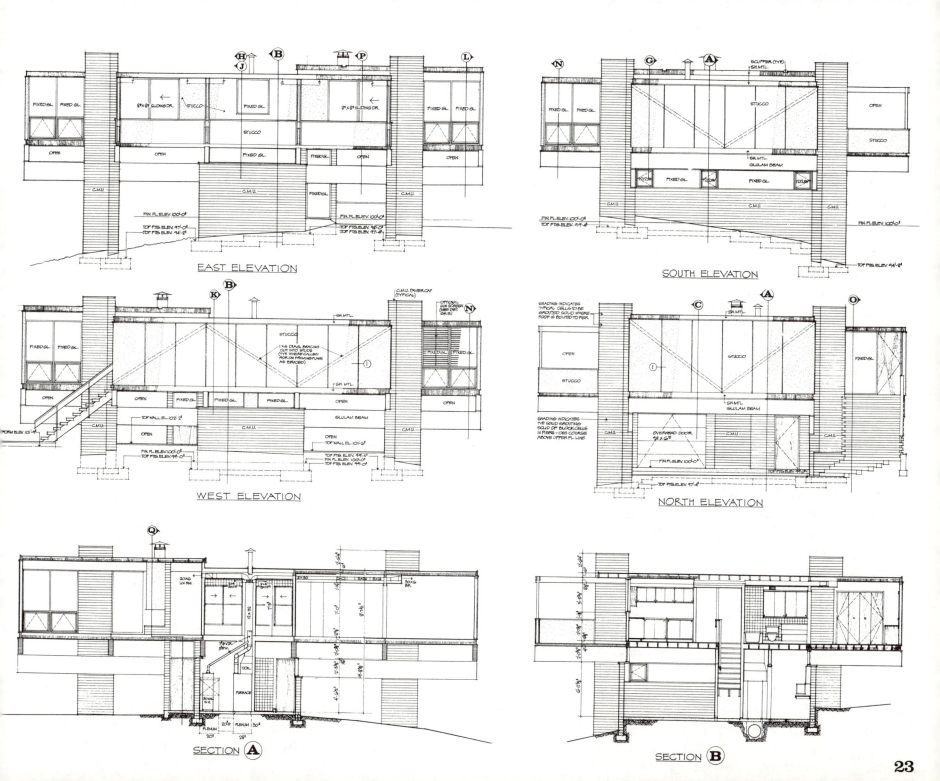

EAST ELEVATION

SOUTH ELEVATION

WEST ELEVATION

NORTH ELEVATION

SECTION A

SECTION B

23

SECTIONAL PERSPECTIVE

The sectional perspective has recently become rather popular as an architectural drawing. History shows ancient examples of this drawing by architects but today it is more often associated with the cutaway views of *Popular Science* or *Mechanics Illustrated*. Much of Paul Rudolph's work has been presented in sectional perspective drawings. The winning entry in the Boston City Hall Competition made excellent use of this drawing.

The reality which perspective adds to a section is very dramatic. The result is a very intimate drawing with which the flat, two-dimensional section can hardly compete. There is the impression that the building, with no little effort, has been cut away especially for the viewer. We have all seen anatomical cutaway drawings, sectional perspectives through beaver lodges and anthills. This drawing is also the view into children's doll houses.

The fact that a particular drawing is widely used and understood by the general public is very significant for architects. We should eagerly use any help in communicating architecture given us by popular usage. For most people, a sectional perspective is much more easily understood than plan, section or elevation. If we intend to communicate clearly, then this is one of the drawings that deserves more extensive use by our profession.

Sectional perspectives are most often projected as one-point perspectives beyond a drafted section. My objections to one-point perspectives voiced under "Perspective" apply just as strongly to sectional perspectives. I find them much less static and more vitally real if constructed along the lines previously described. The rules of taking them through the most characteristic places in the building and looking toward the most interesting ends of the sectioned spaces apply just as they did for sections.

In a multi-storied building it is best to keep the vanishing point at eye level on the ground floor, or principal floor. This means the perspective will look up at the underside of the floors above. While this view will tell little of the floor plan arrangement of the upper floors, it will give a very dramatic view of the floor structure, and with the structural emphasis of contemporary architecture, this is appropriate.

The amount of construction detail you choose to show within the structural thickness of floor, walls and roof is subject to the particulars of each building and drawing. In general, exposed structure looks better in sectional perspectives than do flat furred ceilings. The section through post and beam or waffle slab becomes a vital descriptive line in the drawing. In any case it is best to emphasize the space which is cut through rather than the details within the structural thickness.

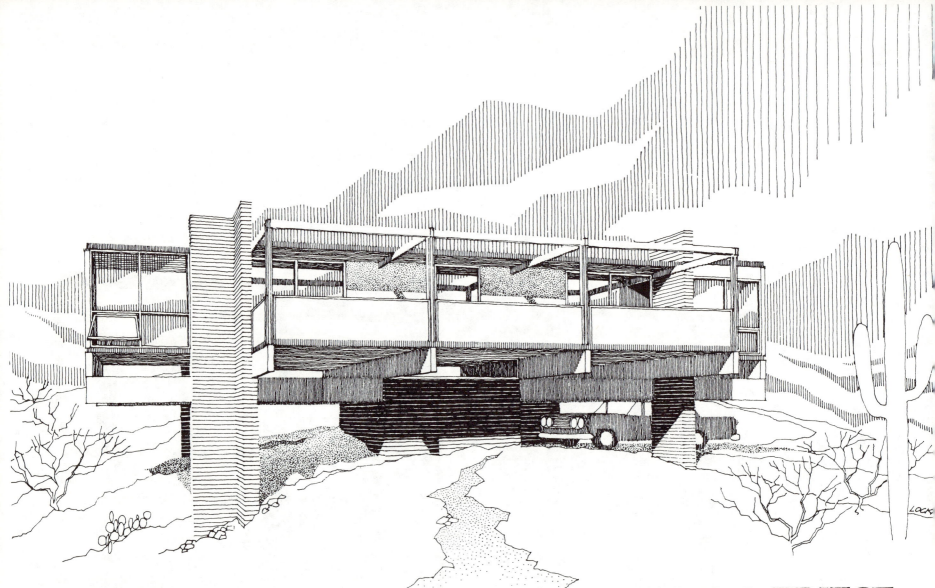

RESIDENCE FOR MR. & MRS. JOHN J. PRIEST

WILLIAM KIRBY LOCKARD
LELAND L. LAWRENCE
Architects

OTHER GRAPHIC MEANS

I think we need some new drawings. The drawings we use in design, and to which I have referred previously as design or presentation drawings, are really no more than incomplete construction drawings. Plan, section and elevation were developed in order to construct a building. This can be demonstrated by the number of symbols and conventions that appear on a set of working drawings which are clearly understood by the construction industry. A center line, the symbol for a door swing, an electrical outlet, the dotted line for overhangs, the dimensioning system, indications for brick and other materials all have to do with communicating how a building is to be built. The only comparable design symbol that comes to mind is the arrow placed at the front door to indicate the main entrance.

To assume that the removal of all these construction symbols makes the drawing an effective design drawing is nonsense. What is needed is a whole new set of drawings with a symbolism of their own. Where the construction drawings are primarily quantitative, these design drawings should be qualitative. They should show how various functions in the building are similar or different, and to what degree. These design drawings could also indicate public and private space, communal and individual space, hard and soft space, dark and light space, and staff and public circulation. With such drawings the architect and his client could more clearly see the reality of any building being designed.

Paul Klee said, "Art does not render the visible; rather it makes visible." This would be exactly the task of the new drawings we need: to make visible systems, relationships and circulation patterns which are not shown by our traditional architectural drawings so that all concerned with the design of a building could better see what they are doing.

Today communication within our profession takes place very quickly, and we all benefit from knowing what other architects are doing to solve problems, problems perhaps similar to ours. Unfortunately what is communicated is often not particularly clear or productive of any in-depth understanding. This is as much the fault of the paucity of means of communication as it is the fault of editorial intent or confusion in the work being published.

Let us take the floor plan as an example. For buildings of a limited scale and simple function the floor plan can be adequately read. But when we take a building of the scale of a 1000-bed general hospital and draw the traditional black and white, mass-void floor plan it is incomprehensible. What comes across is even misleading. Often all that can be seen is an overall formal arrangement of a maze of spaces. The movement paths can be seen, but nothing tells us which corridors are public and which controlled staff corridors. There is no way to read the functional pattern of the hospital. There is a total lack of qualitative indication except by size and relative position.

You may argue that size and relative position of spaces within a composition are the most important means of architectural expression in plan. You may also say that we cannot read this particular complex plan because it is a clumsy inarticulate floor plan and *would* communicate if it were better designed. I agree, but I would ask, "Then, why do we see so many such plans in a profession made up of intelligent, conscientious people?"

I would suggest that one reason is the misleading form of the drawings we use to design a building. Given a standard black and white, mass-void floor plan, the pervasive *gestalt*, the communicated visual image, is the wrong one. The image that comes across is the overall form, which may actually be impossible to experience in any meaningful way, or at least never in the same way as in looking at the floor plan. For example, what is a *pentagon* in floor plan may be a meaningless maze in reality. The seeming order of the overall form belies the real chaos of the plan.

If we habitually used drawings which showed functional patterns, the similarity and difference of functions, the quality or value of the spaces, we would design better buildings. We would worry with these images until they were correct. The problem now is that what we see *seems* ordered when it is not, because of the drawings we use as study tools.

In this section I suggest a few of the more obvious drawings which lie outside the traditional definition of architectural graphics. I am sure there are many others, perhaps more meaningful. One of the first of such "other graphic means" which comes to mind is the tone-coded functional plan. This drawing is sometimes called a "bubble diagram" in our profession—an unfortunately frivolous, degrading name for a potentially important drawing. Planners use a similar tone-code or color-code to make land-use maps. They have discovered that a traditional mass-void plan of a large city is useless in communicating the reality of a large city. The overall functioning of such a complex system is much more quickly understood from a tone-coded land-use map.

The drawing across page is an attempt at such a functional tone-code. The house is the same as that presented earlier in plan, section and elevation. The drawing is an after-the-fact communication and had nothing to do with the design of the house. While this is not the best use of such a drawing, it is still valid as a means of communicating the functioning of the house.

When I tell you that the tone-code is:
BLACK: guests; public
DARK GRAY: food preparation; work and service
LIGHT GRAY: family; communal
WHITE: private; individual sleeping, bathing, dressing
within a few minutes the functional pattern can be seen, more clearly, I believe, than in the plans presented earlier. What also can be seen is that while the floor plan functions very well, its functional pattern really has little to do with the overall symmetry of the form. If I had seen this as clearly as I do now, partly by virtue of this diagram, I might have been able to find a closer relation between functional pattern and overall form.

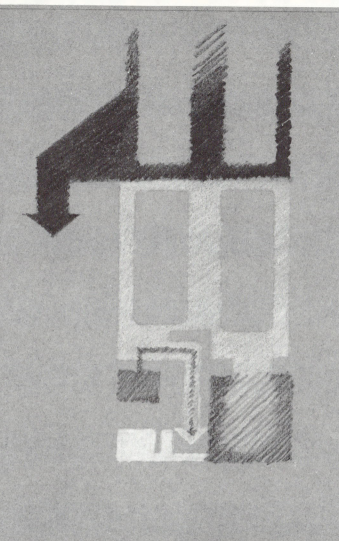

Function: There are many scribbles and doodles concerning function that can be made which will stand prior to any particular architectural form. The fact that any one of these can be translated into a variety of architectural forms seems to prove that this form of drawing is more generic than an architectural floor plan.

To demonstrate a few such doodles let us take the right side of the page to be the public, front, street side of the function. This assumption already preconceives a rectilinear, front-back form which might be avoided with circles or another geometry, but being aware of this, it is a reasonable beginning. The doodles here represent movement paths—functional pattern and points where these movement paths must touch. Black and white lines can indicate frequency and volume and perhaps other qualities by their conformation.

Context: Another plan drawing which is seldom made is a composite drawing of the context into which a building is to be placed. This drawing, in addition to size, shape and topography, could show valued views, prevailing wind, travel of the sun, and existing trees. If the site is urban this composite drawing could also show patterns of pedestrian and vehicular traffic and surrounding buildings in a qualitative as well as a quantitative way. The value of making these drawings lies in being able to see and communicate all of the conditions and pressures existing on a site in one drawing.

Exterior Space: We are accustomed to thinking of our buildings as figures on the ground of the site. In planning groups of buildings or placing a new building into an existing group, it is

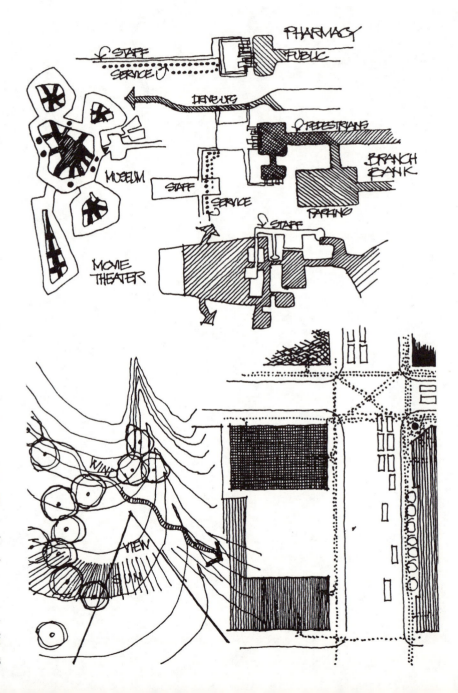

well to try reversing this figure/ground relationship so that the exterior spaces which are being shaped can be better seen.

This last series of plan drawings can perhaps be used only after a plan arrangement is tentatively established. They would be very helpful to test and communicate an order or lack of order in the following qualitative categories.

Lighting: We often use a shadow-cast plan to study and present the three-dimensional form of spaces, assuming a static sun angle. An equally meaningful drawing could be made to show the natural lighting in the spaces related to entry and the proportion of the spaces, at various times of the day.

Privacy: Our buildings are often confusing to the people who populate them in terms of zones or layers of privacy. A single drawing could be made indicating by wall thickness the relative privacy and control of privacy desired in the various spaces. Such a drawing will clearly show the presence or lack of a clear order of privacy.

Texture: Another drawing can be found to indicate texture of finishes in richness, imperviousness, or visual-tactile stimulation. This order is perhaps secondary but a drawing could show whether it correctly reinforces, destroys or makes equivocal the other orders.

Beyond the plan we can find other uses of drawing in designing, analyzing and communicating a building. The opportunities also exist in section, elevation and perspective.

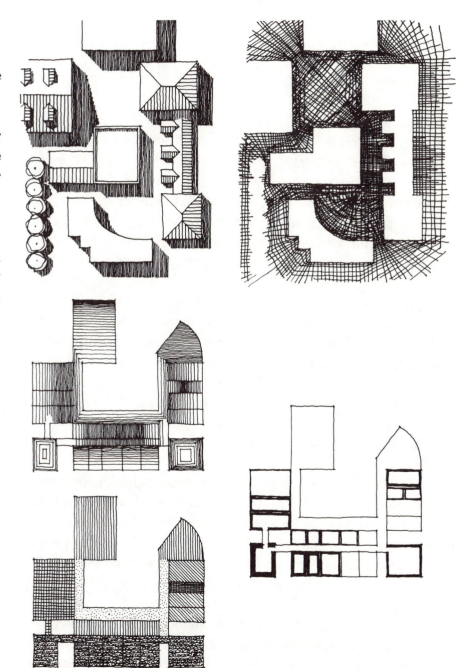

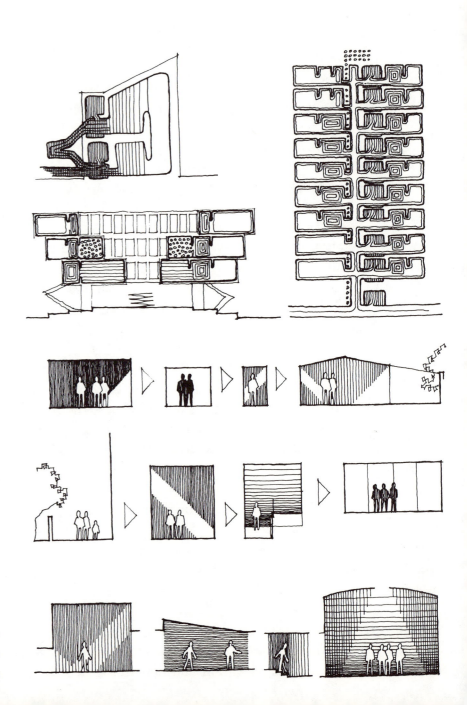

Vertical Function: Functional diagrams should be extended vertically in a multilevel building. Just as they may be seen more clearly in a diagram plan, so can they best be studied vertically in a diagram that emphasizes the difference and order of human activities. Such a diagram can study and show potentials for vertical connections and interpenetrations of space, and the order or lack of it in the spatial stacking.

Sequence: Another opportunity for drawing might be an analysis of sequence in a series of diagrammatic sections. The sections could indicate the cross section of the movement path in relation to the human figure and whether the space was lighted unilaterally, bilaterally, from above, behind, or in front. Such a series of drawings would show if there was any order or interest in the shaping and lighting of a sequence. Does the light source change? in relation to what? are the changes meaningful?

Another series of sections could be made longitudinally along the movement path. Here the same qualities of size, shape and lighting would reveal the articulation of the difference between transition spaces and collection, arrival spaces. Are the transition spaces shaped directionally? Are the arrival spaces emphasized by their sectional form and the way they are lighted?

Metaphor: The search for meaning and symbol in architecture treads a complex, difficult path. We have almost lost any sense of formal propriety. The dome and the bell tower stand as

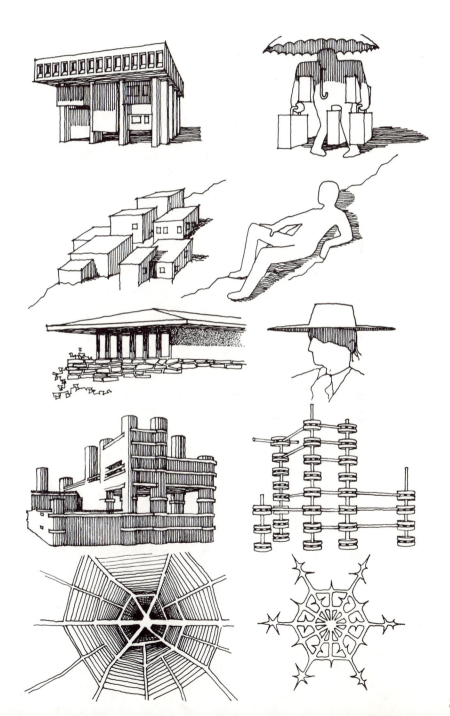

lonely survivors of other ages when architectural forms had a broad general meaning, and even they are confused today. We have switched the symbolic death-life-heaven's canopy, religious mystery of the dome to the often equally unclear mystery of government. Perhaps we will even find a better way than overall form to communicate our intentions.

This is a dangerous area for drawing. The tightrope above maudlin sentimentality and obvious vulgarism is difficult to negotiate. But as in most endeavors the greatest rewards lie where the risks are greatest.

Architects often use verbal metaphors in speaking of architectural form. Frank Lloyd Wright used the cupping and praying attitudes of hands metaphorically to describe two of his churches. There may be some question as to the appropriateness of a metaphor, but the efficiency and clarity of the metaphor as a way of knowing and communicating is undeniable. A building can stand, or lie, or hover, or burrow, in response to a site. A building can open its arms or turn its back. A building can be comfortably casual or stiffly formal. A building can overpower, open onto, lead, contain.

Graphic metaphors communicate more than verbal metaphors. If we used them to communicate our intentions in architecture they could lead to a return of meaning in our environment.

Although the tools with which we draw do not deserve the dominance they enjoy in the traditional categorizing of all drawings as *pen and ink, pencil,* or *charcoal,* the habit of drawing with a line-making tool continues to exert a tremendous influence in conceptual diagramming. Line-making tools like pens, pencils and markers demand that we draw distinctions or dividers between spaces instead of relationships. In plan or section these spatial dividers become walls or ceilings and floors, and we fix our attention on these and their patterns and configurations rather than on the patterns and configurations of the spaces they enclose.

This may seem to be a nit-picking distinction and it can be objected that we really sketch both the spaces and the spatial dividers simultaneously and can quite easily learn to perceive both equally. Based on what we know about perceptual dominance, however, as in figure/field ambiguity, I doubt that they can ever be perceived equally. The difference can be easily tested and appreciated by drawing space directly with a white prismacolor pencil on dark paper. This is particularly valuable as a sensitizing experience and I think the perceptual difference in whether you draw the solids or the voids will be immediately apparent.

The availability and habitual use of different colors or tones in making conceptual sketches will soon raise their level of sophistication. We have been defined as meaning-seeking or meaning-making animals, and in a few moments of sketching with only two different colors or tones the sketcher will begin to make their visual difference meaningful. The difference will quickly become qualitatively categorical— functionally as in the drawing on page 29, or perhaps contextually or spatially—and subsequent sketches will thus present much more information to the designer in their added levels of meaning.

Our cultural heritage is dominated by a linear, verbal, "rational" tradition which can inhibit the use of drawing in design. In its most narrow interpretation, our verbal cultural indoctrination implies that we should, or in fact do, represent alternative courses of action to ourselves verbally and then make decisions based on these verbal or "rational" alternatives. I do not decide or act like this and I have difficulty believing that anyone does, or should—particularly designers of a physical environment which will be perceived through a set of senses dominated by pre-verbal, pre-rational (or supra-verbal, supra-rational) vision.

Acceptance of the verbal or "rational" model of the mind implies that all conception occurs, or should occur, in the verbal mode and then the hand in drawing simply "prints out" the verbal decisions. This way of thinking about the role of drawing in design inhibits the expectancy which should accompany conceptual sketching. Design drawings should be made in anticipation and confidence that design opportunities will appear *in the drawings* that were not preconceived.

One of the strongest arguments for maximizing the use of drawing in design is that drawing is one of the best ways to allow the unconscious mind to contribute to the process. We are much older, and perhaps much wiser, than our mathematical, verbal, "rational" left frontal lobes, and drawing is one of the most natural and direct outlets for this rich and mysterious resource. We should habitually pursue a vigorous experimentation with our conceptual graphics and expect to see and learn to recognize opportunities in the patterns and relationships which *appear* in the drawings we make.

I believe most architects are, and should be, *visual* decision-makers, and the verbal arguments which they use in explanation and persuasion are all after-the-fact rationalizations. In such visual decision-making, what we show our older, wiser, pre-verbal, holistic mind is extremely important; and since visual decision-making is quickly prejudiced, the order in which we make drawn representations of whatever we are designing is also very important. Instead of limiting our exploratory drawings to plan section and elevation and further assuming that particular order of making the drawings, we should habitually invent new ways of representing our designs to ourselves based on the particular design task or on the concept we are proposing.

We are further inhibited in using and thinking about drawing by the particular part of our cultural heritage which categorizes drawings. Drawings are normally categorized according to their form (plan, section, elevation, perspective, etc.), which we inherit from drafting, and their media (charcoal, pencil, ink etc.), which we inherit from art. Two much more meaningful ways for designers to think about the drawings they make are in terms of two relationships:

the drawing's relationship to reality
and
the drawing's relationship to the design process

To assume that the conventional architectural drawings have any necessary or exclusive relationship either to reality or to the design process is to forfeit one of the richest potentials you have for seeing a problem in a uniquely different way or for escaping the prejudices and preconceptions that plague any familiar process.

GENERATIVE DOODLES

One of the main thoughts in this book is that the importance of architectural drawing dwindles as the drawing becomes more refined. Yet in surveying the drawings I have used to illustrate my ideas I find that they are all rather stiff, studied works. This is a natural response to the formality of publishing — like the interviewed person who is shocked into an over-inhibited speechless state when he finds he is on television. It may even be necessary to reach some degree of finish with the drawings in order to prove myself worthy of saying something to the reader.

Further, I have never habitually saved the first rough sketches precisely because they are only means — their only value being an interim visual statement toward a final real building. The rough sketches on this page, however, I have saved. I reproduce them here, full size, to show the first sketches from which the following series of drawings concerning techniques developed.

Except for the need to communicate the architectural idea more formally to other people, the purpose for drawing the space is fulfilled with these little sketches. They were made on the back of a sheet of the program during the annual president's breakfast at the University of Arizona with a fountain pen among other notes and doodles. On any basis, for time, ink, paper, or effort expended compared to value gained, they are the most valuable drawings in this book.

THE TECHNIQUES

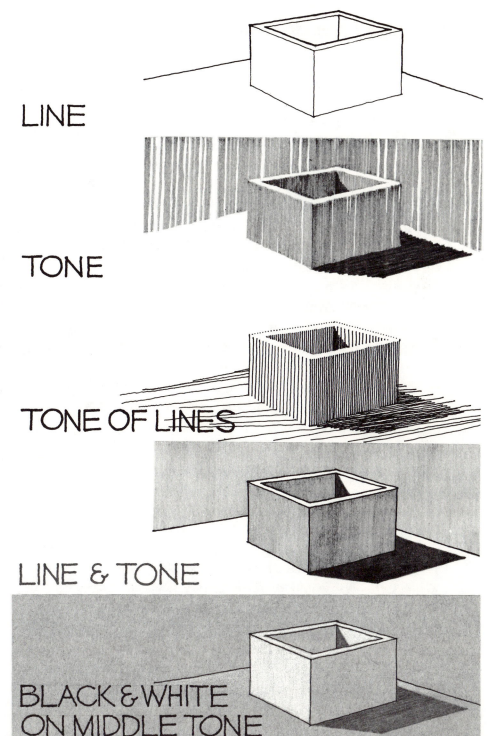

LINE

TONE

TONE OF LINES

LINE & TONE

BLACK & WHITE
ON MIDDLE TONE

Analyses of drawing techniques are often based on the drawing instrument used. This has always seemed a little implement-minded to me and not nearly as generic as the following basis which I think stands behind any question of tools.

There are two pure drawing techniques: *line* and *tone*. All the rest are combinations of these two. A line drawing delineates objects by their outlines in space and indicates planar intersections by lines. A more sophisticated line drawing will also indicate texture by line. A tone drawing depends on the contrast between one tone and another to depict objects in space. Edges and planar intersections are indicated by changes in tone. The tone drawing is truer to the way we perceive forms in space. The line drawing is an abstraction, replacing the virtual lines that are formed between contrasting tones with actual lines.

I believe that line drawing is the best technique for architectural drawing. Architecture is real and definitive, not amorphous, and this quality of being seems best described by linear drawing. Construction working drawings must be drawn in line, and so we are committed to the linear technique in architectural practice. Line drawing is flexible: you can hang all sorts of color, tone, and texture variations on the frame of a strong drawing technique.

LINE DRAWINGS

The essence of a line is its continuousness. A line should be drawn in one continuous motion, not in a series of short fuzzy strokes. Confidence in drawing lines can be accomplished only by drawing them many, many times. One exercise that may be useful is to connect pairs of dots spaced long distances apart with one line, drawn continuously, freehand. If unsure, draw a very light line first, then correct it with a heavier line.

In a pure line drawing the variation in the visual weight of the line becomes the only means of expression. This may be accomplished with the density of the line, as with diluted inks, or with the thickness, as with sizes of pens. The greater this variation in line weight, the more interesting the drawing, *provided there is discernible meaning behind the variations*. Since the means of architectural composition is space, it seems clear that the means of expression in architectural drawing should be used to speak a spatial language.

I have found the following hierarchy of line weights to be meaningful:

Heaviest line: indicates a slice in space; the profile or roof line against the sky would be an infinitely deep spatial slice and should have a heavy outline. The weight of other profiles depends on how far they lie in front of their background. The deeper the slice in space, the heavier the outline.

Medium line: use to indicate *intersections* of planes, such as inside and outside corners; intersections of ceiling and wall or floor and wall.

Light line: use to indicate lines that occur *on* a plane, indicating no change in space such as a brick joint, wood grain, etc.

Textured line: use to indicate carpet, grass, pebbles, marble. This is really a type of light line (above) occurring on a plane, but special because its configuration indicates a texture.

This hierarchy is overlaid with another hierarchy — that of closeness to the viewer. For instance, if an infinitely deep spatial slice occurs in the far distance, its weight would be diminished by that distance.

Be careful to understand what it is you are drawing with each line. It may be an edge, an intersection, or a specific texture, but you should be aware of exactly what it is you are representing with each line. Students often spend great amounts of time drawing purposeless lines. If a surface is really smooth and characterless, don't be afraid to leave it so in the drawing. Beware of lines which begin nowhere and end nowhere. Each line should begin with a definite relationship to another line and go to another definite relationship with still another line. The lines need this connectedness or they become arbitrary and can be imagined to be pushed around on the surface of the drawing. All lines should actually touch one another at their ends except those which fade out at the edges of the drawing. The entire network of lines which is the drawing should be imagined to be joined together like a hairnet or a spider's web so that if you could pick up one end of a line you could lift the entire network off the page. Any loose lines that do not adhere to this network are superfluous.

TONE DRAWINGS

This way of drawing is the most realistic (the least abstract). It defines forms in space by difference in value, which is the same way we perceive them in reality. The line, as the profile line around an object, does not exist here except as a *virtual* line which divides a darker tone from a lighter one.

The establishing of these virtual lines becomes very critical. They cannot all be of equal importance. That is, the tonal difference between a wall and a floor at their intersection is not the same as the tonal difference between a bell tower and the sky beyond, or the tonal difference between shadow and sunlight. To differentiate between the importance of the various virtual lines, we impose a hierarchy on the technique.

The strongest virtual line in tone rendering would be that created between black and white. This maximum contrast line should be reserved for the deepest spatial slice or the line between sunlight and shadows. This hierarchy corresponds to that for *line* drawings in the previous exercise. Considerable planning is necessary to assure that in a complicated overlapping of forms you do not run out of tonal differences before you run out of forms. Tone drawing has always been, until recently the finest type of architectural rendering. For years it was done with ink wash — the tones being built up by many applications of a wash of the same value.

Under the hand of such masters as Ted Kautzky and Hugh Ferriss, pencil tone rendering gradually replaced ink wash. Perhaps an even more important influence in the change from a wet to dry technique was that pencil tone takes less equipment and time, is easily done in an office, can be done on tracing paper and blueprinted. Another factor which contributed to the popularity of pencil tone rendering is that under Kautzky it became a technique of great character, showing each pencil stroke, which was uniquely appropriate to the architectural materials of that time — stone, brick, shake shingles.

Today, pencil tone rendering is losing popularity for several reasons. It is more demanding in time and talent than other techniques and it is somewhat inappropriate to today's materials — glass, steel, aluminum, formica — which are rather slick and characterless from edge to edge, thus indicating line technique.

The tone drawing on the facing page appears softer or weaker than the previous line drawing. It was printed by the half-tone process, which uses screens in the photography of the original drawing. This changes the tones to relatively sparse or relatively dense areas of tiny dots. Even a line reproduced in this way will be printed as a line of dots — thus the softer quality of the drawing.

TONE OF LINES DRAWINGS

This way of drawing is actually a tone drawing, similar in principle to the preceding tone drawing. The difference lies in the fact that the tones are made of lines, the various spacing of the lines producing the relative value of the tones. The edges of the tones are established by the virtual lines indicated by the ends of the lines.

You will notice that the background wall was changed from brick to wood. The material change was made because, like most techniques, the tone of lines is more suited to certain materials than others, and to wood more than brick.

Difference in line weight is of no importance in a tone of lines drawing. Each line is as important as any other, like a single brick in a wall. Direction of lines, however, becomes quite important. Render walls and other vertical surfaces with vertical lines. Render ceilings, floors, and other horizontal surfaces with lines running *across* the picture, from side to side. *Never* render horizontal planes with lines running to a vanishing point within the perspective. When this is done it calls entirely too much attention to the vanishing point. One of the aims in drawing an architectural space is to allow the viewer's eye to linger, move around the space and see it all. If you indicate strongly or emphasize in any way the position of a vanishing point the viewer's eye will go into that hole and never come back. And besides, that little point represents infinity, and the prospect of seeing infinity is as ridiculous as it is tempting.

The sketches below, hopefully, show the danger of emphasizing the vanishing point. There may be times when it is actually desirable to pull the viewer's eye down a particular path. But this will always be to the detriment of the rest of the drawing.

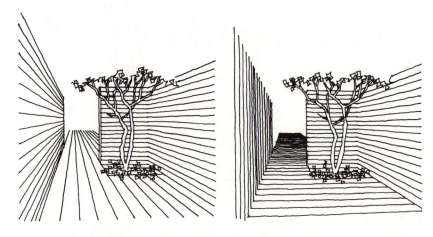

The engraving of United States currency is basically a tone of lines technique. This technique is also used by two very influential contemporary delineators—Paul Rudolph and Davis Bité. They generally use drafted lines and build up tones with cross-hatched layers of parallel lines at various angles. Mr. Rudolph is one of the few architects of note today who still does his own presentation drawings — beautifully.

This technique is one of the best for reduction to small scale. A good tone of lines drawing can be reduced to postcard size and it will be spectacular, the detail still there.

LOCKARD 66

LINE AND TONE DRAWINGS

This is a combination technique and both line and tone give up a little of their character in the combination.

Since variation in tone can be used to indicate position in space, the hierarchy of line weights, so important in a pure line drawing, is of less importance in a line and tone drawing. And since lines can be used to indicate texture and surface character, the tones may and should be flat, smooth, characterless tints. The tones may be colored washes or sheets of perfectly even texture. ("Zip-A-Tone" and other manufactured products may be used.) This combination technique is the basic technique of the two most influential architectural renderers of recent years: Helmut Jacoby and Gordon Cullen. Jacoby uses flat colored tones or textured tones in combination with extremely detailed line drafting. Cullen uses the same technique except that his drawings are entirely freehand. This is an excellent example of how two men using the same technique of depicting three-dimensional space can still communicate in completely different ways. Jacoby's drawings are overwhelming in their precision and painstaking detail. You have probably seen his drawings for "Armstrong's" ceiling products or his renderings for leading architects. Cullen, on the other hand, is loose and free while remaining definitive and responsible. The best collection of his sketches is in his book, *Townscape.*

The important point is that both Jacoby and Cullen use line drawing to hold the combination together, and both their techniques are clearly *drawing* techniques — not painting techniques.

Line and tone is also the technique of many cartoonists and "pop" artists. It is exactly the technique of children's coloring books, and the rules are about the same — stay within the lines and make it as even as you can.

In applying the tone to the drawing across page, I have introduced another rule which may seem to contradict some of what I have said before. Under the last technique, tone of lines, I suggested rendering vertical surfaces with vertical lines and horizontal surfaces with horizontal lines running from side to side, not to the vanishing point. The application of a tone should not follow this vertical-horizontal rule.

The tones should be perfectly even if possible. In the drawing across page the tones were applied with a pencil and in spite of much effort it is possible to see the directional quality or stroking of the application. In this technique, this stroking or grain should all be the same, vertical I think, regardless of whether the surface is horizontal or vertical.

This technique is a shortcut. It is like beginning in the middle and going in opposite directions at once. Instead of beginning with an empty white piece of paper and proceeding to black, laboriously building up all the in-between tones, you start on a broad gray middle base and have only to add the whites and the blacks.

The first several attempts at drawing in this technique may not, and actually may never, take less time. The beauty of the technique lies in the economy, if not of time, of means. The actual rendered areas of black and white model with impressive economy the three-dimensional space in light.

One excellent collection of drawings in this style can be found in the Royal Barry Wills book, *Houses For the Budgeteer*, some of which were done by Hugh Stubbins. The background color may be rather strong in chroma. Wills' book uses a rather green green. Generally it is best to reserve the whites for those surfaces in direct sunlight and use the blacks and dark tones to delineate those areas in shade. The darkest blacks are best reserved for shadows.

This is the pure form of the technique used on buff tracing paper throughout this book, and which I always use in design sketching. With a white-colored pencil and pen or pencil it models forms and surfaces in light more quickly than any technique I know.

This technique is really a whole new category and not correctly comparable to others in this series. This is true because tone drawings, tone of lines and line and tone drawings can all be done as black and white on middle tone. The drawing across page is a line and tone drawing.

You may have seen chalk or pastel drawings done on middle tone backgrounds. Both Degas and Toulouse-Lautrec did what (for me) are some of their freshest sketches in this technique. Pastel portraitists often use a middle tone background. The whites or light tones come up off the surface in a way not quite possible with other techniques.

As an architectural drawing technique, it has the disadvantage of not being reproducible. Even when done on buff tracing paper as described above and illustrated in the series following THE OVERLAY (pages 82 and 84), it cannot be successfully blueprinted because the colored pencil tones all print blue. And so it is an elegant one-of-a-kind drawing technique, and as such, doomed to limited use where reproduction is required.

DIAZO PROCESS PRINTS

The most common method of reproducing architectural drawings is the Diazo process by which most working drawings are printed. The process is commonly called "blueprinting" although that name is an incorrect carryover from a much earlier process. The Diazo process is very economical both in terms of materials and time and many architectural offices own their own printing machines.

In the first stage of the process the print paper, which is coated with a light-sensitive chemical, is overlaid with a drawing on tracing paper and then slowly rotated around a cylindrical high-intensity light. The second stage develops the exposed paper by passing it slowly through the fumes of a chemical which causes a reaction of the light-sensitive coating. The entire background area of the print is thus fully exposed to both light and fumes, and the combination burns away the chemical coating so that at the normally slow exposure speed the entire background of the print remains white. The areas of the print which were protected from light exposure by the ink or graphite lines and tones of the drawing, however, are turned *black* or *blue* or *sepia* by the fumes, depending on the color of print paper used.

By increasing the speed during the first or *exposure* stage of the process, you can obtain a print which has an even tone of gray, blue or sepia over the entire background of the print, and the intensity of this tone can be very finely tuned by slight adjustments in the speed control. This technological ability to make such vast and variable tones shortcuts the most time-consuming visual interest category in drawing— *tonal interest.* The Diazo process can do in moments what it would otherwise take hours to accomplish.

There are several ways of using this technological tone-making ability to save time and raise the quality of architectural presentation drawings. The four drawings which follow are color-separation reproductions of actual sepia prints, colored with prismacolor pencils to achieve various purposes. The drawing across page and the following one on page 51 are reproductions of prints of the tracing paper original of the LINE AND TONE drawing on page 45 and show two alternative approaches to coloring sepia prints.

When a drawing like that on page 45 is run through the Diazo process at a speed fast enough to produce the background tones seen across page, the original range of tones is compressed. The effect is very much like putting on a pair of sepia-colored glasses. What was a tonal range of from white to very dark gray is reduced or compressed to a range of from middle-tone sepia to very dark sepia. What needs to be done in the coloring of such a print is to restore the highlights— the values on the light side of gray. This is why colors lighter or whiter than the background tone are most effective.

The illustration across page demonstrates one way of coloring a sepia print which suggests a full color rendering without making any design commitment to specific colors. There are times when such an approach is honest and useful in communicating the spatial and material qualities of a space without prematurely getting into color selection. A client or collaborator can hardly object to blue sky, green trees and grass and neutral white indications of sunlit surfaces. The Prismacolor pencils used were: WHITE 938, SKY BLUE 919, APPLE GREEN 912 and OLIVE GREEN 911.

The illustration across page demonstrates a full color approach to coloring an identical sepia print. This way of coloring risks objection by your client or collaborator in the personally subjective area of color preference, but the risk must be taken if we are to communicate our designs honestly.

One interim alternative between full color rendering and the neutral color application shown on the preceding page would have been to color only the *architectural* surfaces; in this case the brick, since the raw sepia will represent the wood very well. This would have perhaps been safer and would have honestly communicated the dominant color of the architectural space without risking rejection based on a dislike of yellow and orange upholstery colors. I have chosen, however, to jump ahead to include the colors of the furnishings to demonstrate the value of simple bold color schemes in the choice of secondary, non-architectural colors.

I discovered the use of colored sepia prints while I was working with Nicholas Sakellar and the prints are known around Tucson as "Sakellar specials." I'm sure that we were not the first to use sepia prints for presentation drawings. They were probably discovered earlier and rather simultaneously everywhere the Diazo process is used. Their greatest advantages are that they offer a short cut to tonal interest and they allow you to make multiple prints while retaining the original drawings.

Note that the "unitness" of the individual bricks in the floor and the individual brick courses in the walls is emphasized in the original LINE AND TONE drawing on page 45. It takes only a few minutes to apply a slightly different tone to a few individual units in any composite architectural surface and thus communicate the dominant visual characteristic of such surfaces. This "unitness" can be further emphasized in coloring prints by applying slightly different colors to different bricks or courses, as has been done in the illustration across page.

Many architectural materials, like brick, have a color richness that can never be represented satisfactorily with any single color. The coloring of the brick across page was applied in two coats: first Prismacolor ORANGE 918 and then CRIMSON LAKE 925. Both coats were randomly varied in intensity so that the richness and variety of the color approaches that of a real brick wall.

The palette of colors which you use in making architectural drawings should be very carefully selected. I use a very restricted set of colors sorted out over years of sketching. One of the surest signs of a fledgling colorist is the Easter Egg look of their architectural renderings. Simple color schemes are the most effective and one of the advantages of sepia prints is that the overall sepia tone dominates and holds together the entire drawing.

EXTERIOR PERSPECTIVES

Choice of view is perhaps the most critical opportunity in any perspective. Most exterior perspectives back away so far, to get one glorious all-encompassing view, that they lose any sense of the texture or joinery of the building. Exterior perspectives are much better taken from one of the defined exterior spaces of the building, like the one across page. Multilevel spaces like the present perspective are always best drawn from the lower level because the stairs which make the level change are in full view. Figure groups on both levels also help explain the various levels, but be careful to keep some figures on the lower viewer's eye level.

The sun angle and the placement of the shadow pattern it casts is the next most important opportunity in drawing exterior perspectives. You should be responsible to draw rather characteristic sun angles rather than, say, the shadow pattern at 5 a.m. on June 22. Within the normal range of sun angles, however, you should choose the one which casts the most interesting or descriptive shadows.

The traditional compositional categories of foreground, middleground and background are also important for exterior perspectives. The building, like the featured object in any composition, normally occupies the middleground and needs a believable, complementary context: a foreground and a background.

Figure groups, trees and plants and exterior furniture are all important in any foreground. They should be placed carefully to demonstrate the space of the foreground and indicate its scale and use without obscuring important intersections of the space-defining surfaces. The ground plane of the foreground is the first place to indicate texture in an exterior perspective. The careful rendering of this receding textured plane will do more than anything to make the space of the foreground read.

Background can be indicated simply by drawing receding layers of space beyond and behind the building. Wherever possible, these layers should disappear and reappear behind the building, other objects, or themselves. This *layering* is the main purpose of both the foreground and background and does more than anything else to extend the space of the perspective.

In developing the foreground and background, care should be taken not to shift the emphasis away from the architecture. This can be assured by leaving the figures, trees or furniture under-rendered and ghostlike and concentrating the tones and colors on the architectural surfaces. You may further de-emphasize the figures, furniture or even trees by casting no shadows from them as in the movie, *Last Year at Marianbad*.

One of the great advantages of sepia prints of exterior perspectives is the opportunity they offer for rendering the reflectivity of water and glass. The interior detail seen through the glass and the darker reflections should all be put on *before* the print is run. After the print is run, the light blue sky reflection can be applied with vertical strokes *over* the indications of the interior. This layering effect offered by colored prints represents the reflective layer of glass more easily than any technique I know of.

NIGHT PERSPECTIVES

Many buildings are used as much or even more after dark than they are in daylight, yet we seldom see design drawings which study or indicate the nighttime experience of the environment. One of the reasons is that the effort required to build up dark night tones from white paper by normal methods is out of the question. One alternative is to make night renderings on dark colored board, but this requires transferring what is probably a tracing paper perspective to an opaque board, which you may not want to take the time to do. The Diazo process allows you to overcome these difficulties and make night perspectives as the rather easy fall-out of the process of making any daytime perspective on tracing paper.

By running a Diazo process print at a very high speed, a very dark background tone may be obtained all over the print. If you order such a print from a commercial blueprinter, it may be difficult to persuade the machine operator to run it fast enough, since it will be hard for him to imagine the usefulness of so dark a print. If you are using the same drawing for a similar daytime rendering, the making of the print for the night rendering will require some planning, since it should be run before you cast the shadows or draw reflections on the glass.

After the print is made, you simply "turn on the lights" and render the interior spaces as brightly illuminated, with light from them washing out onto surfaces such as patio floors and walls which extend out from the illuminated interiors. Knowing the orientations of the various surfaces to the sources of artificial illumination, you may strengthen the night rendering by going ahead and toning those surfaces dark which will be turned away from the artificial night lighting and still be

consistent with the sun assumption of the eventual daylight rendering. In the drawing across page, all the shade tones were applied before the print was made. Aside from these tones the entire tonal range of the night rendering will be applied after the print is made with very light colored pencils. Landscape lighting, underwater pool lights, lighted windows in distant buildings, and stars will also help convey the impression of an after dark environment.

Another reason for the lack of night perspectives may be that conventional architectural drawing courses deal only with daylight and the casting of shadows from the single light source of the sun. Although the patterns of illumination from the multiple light sources of artificial illumination can be quite complex, this is no excuse for avoiding the making of study drawings and presentation drawings which represent, if in somewhat simplified form, artificial lighting. Such drawings are not that difficult to make and our profession's recognition of Mr. Edison's invention in the drawings with which we study and present our designs seems long overdue.

Throughout this book I have tried to emphasize the honest, open drawings a designer makes for himself which are by all measures the most important drawings; but for a moment let's just consider the public relations or persuasive value of an additional night perspective made as the bonus fall out of the process that produces the normally mandatory daylight perspective. Your having taken the trouble to study and present *both* a day and night perspective of a client's building is bound to be impressive in terms of the apparent human effort involved, and the concealment of the ease with which it was produced is not nearly as dishonest as the artificial complexity with which some other professions try to impress us.

REPRODUCTION PROCESSES

An architect needs to have a working knowledge of the reproduction processes by which drawings can be printed in newspapers or brochures. If you are particular about the drawings which communicate your work then you must know the technology of reproduction much as you must know and respond to the construction technology which will build your buildings. This will be brought home to you the first time you invest a great effort in drawing a building of which you are very proud and have its reproduction botched.

The best way to learn the reproduction process is to hand-carry your drawings through the first few times and learn the people as well as the mechanics of the process. In this way you will begin to become as familiar with other reproduction processes as you are with blueprinting.

The sight of an apprentice draftsman waiting eagerly by the Ozalid machine while the blueprint boy runs his first tracing is really touching. The lesson learned by this first experience with reproduction is always clear — nothing magic happens in that machine (or in any reproduction process). If the quality is not there on the original drawing, neither will it be there on the print.

What can happen in a reproduction process, however, is that the quality which does exist in the original can be very much reduced or garbled unless the process is understood, and the delineator's intentions made clear to the people involved in the reproduction. My experience has been that the incorrect choice of line cut or half-tone or the fiendish cropping of a perspective are seldom the result of any deliberate malice toward the delineator. These atrocities are more often decisions made in re-

sponse to expediency in the absence of any instructions by the author of the drawing.

As an example of the intricacies of a printing process, let's take the BLACK AND WHITE ON MIDDLE TONE drawing on page 47. Although it is meant to represent a drawing on middle tone paper using pen and ink, a white Prismacolor pencil, and an ordinary lead pencil, the drawing was reproduced in a quite different way.

Overprinting a colored paper with white ink is very difficult in ordinary offset printing because white inks which approach the opacity needed to cover a colored paper would be so thick they would gum up the high speed presses. In addition to this difficulty, it is more economical to begin with cheaper white paper and print a background color over the entire paper *except* in the areas which would be colored white in such a drawing as is being represented. In offset printing it is "times through the press" that counts; it is more economical in this case to print 80% of a page of white paper a color than to try to print 20% of a page of colored paper white.

The drawings from which page 47 was produced were quite different than the drawing they were meant to represent would have been. There had to be a separate drawing—in red Prismacolor (because it photographs well)—of the areas to be left white in the final page. This drawing was made as a tracing paper overlay of the base drawing and the two kept in very careful alignment. A halftone negative of this drawing was then made and from that an offset plate which printed the background color.

THE MATERIALS OF ARCHITECTURE

SPACE

Lately the banner of space as an architectural material has been carried high. If anything, I think it should be lowered slightly or at least more correctly understood. The quality and character of architectural space is dependent on, and inseparable from, the surfaces which bound the space. Space cannot exist alone and we cannot yet reasonably enclose it with a uniform characterless material. So there is nothing like pure space, or a purely spatial approach to architecture. We perceive space by seeing its bounding surfaces and we communicate space by drawing these same surfaces.

I've talked about spatial emphasis in drawing under "The Techniques" and will again under "Emphasis." What remains to be said here regarding the drawing of space as an architectural material has to do with the order in which design drawings are made. If we believe space is an important architectural material and that the quality of the spaces of a building amount to its architectural quality, should we not begin by drawing the spaces?

I realize this is heresy. "When you are drawing the floor plan you should be thinking spatially, in three or four dimensions"— "they sold the client a pretty picture, and now we are going to have to figure out how to build it." These are but two quotations, the first from teachers, the second from chief draftsmen, that you have heard or will hear ere you have long been in the profession of architecture. They both promote the idea and ridicule the alternatives of drawing the traditional construction drawings — plan, section and elevation — in that order and in great detail and then only later, in what time is left, curiously drawing the spaces which result.

My only question is why not start with the spaces? Why not begin with the desired quality or the qualitative alternatives of the major spaces, and then decide by what sequence and in what relation these spaces are served and connected for entry to other spaces? I do not advocate that these be the only drawings, but that they can very reasonably be the first. The shape of a sanctuary and how that space is lighted to house and illuminate the liturgy seems the reasonable way to begin to design a church. The shape of a living room or family room and how it is entered and lighted may be a reasonable way to begin the design of a home.

The only objection I can find to this approach is that it may result in a fragmented collection of spaces which has no overall formal order. And this is exactly where I would like to force the issue. What kind of an overall formal order should a spatially designed building obey? If we are designing with space as an architectural material then the order must be one perceived from within the spaces and the sequence of them, not from outside.

The order we perceive from overall plan, section and elevation, is an entirely different thing. It is an order which may have nothing to do with the spatial experience of the building. It is an order which may be perceived by migrating geese but not by the people who must find their way through the building.

LIGHT

Light is as surely an architectural material as space or the conventional building materials. An architect builds containers for people, space and light. In drawing architectural space, the designer should habitually draw and study how that space will be revealed by light. This practice should be habitual from the first sketches so that light becomes a determinant in design, not just a presentation device.

Shadow-casting is conventionally taught in plan and elevation as a rigid two-dimensional pattern-making which leaves the student with a fragmented understanding of what actually happens when sunlight falls on three-dimensional forms. This practice is another of the subsidies conferred on the orthographic projections by traditional architectural education. I am sure shadow casting is much more clearly taught and understood in perspective, where the entire three-dimensional pattern can be comprehended.

In architectural shadow-casting, we assume three light conditions: sun, shadow and shade. Sun and shadow can occur side by side on the same surface, but surfaces which are turned away from the sun in shade will have neither sun nor shadow. The line which separates sun and shade, except in inside corners, is the line which casts the shadow, and we will call it the *casting line*.

In this brief introduction to light we will only consider shadows cast by and on rectangular objects. In such a rectangular world only two relationships are possible between the line which casts any shadow and the surface on which the shadow falls: *perpendicular* and *parallel*.

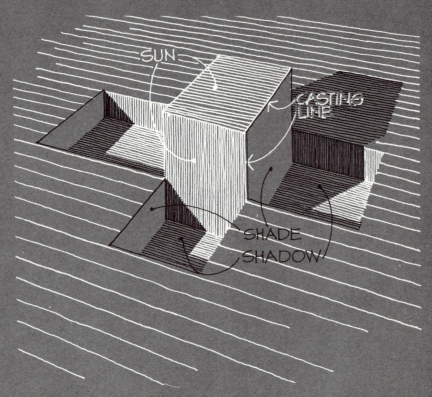

In the *perpendicular* relationship, both the angle of the shadow and the ratio of casting line length to shadow length will vary dramatically throughout the day, but at any moment all similar perpendicular relationships will cast shadows which are parallel and which have the same ratio of casting line length to shadow length.

Parallel shadows follow a much tighter set of rules. Because the sun's rays are parallel, all shadows of a casting line which is parallel to the surface on which the shadow falls, will be parallel to and exactly the same length as the line which casts them.

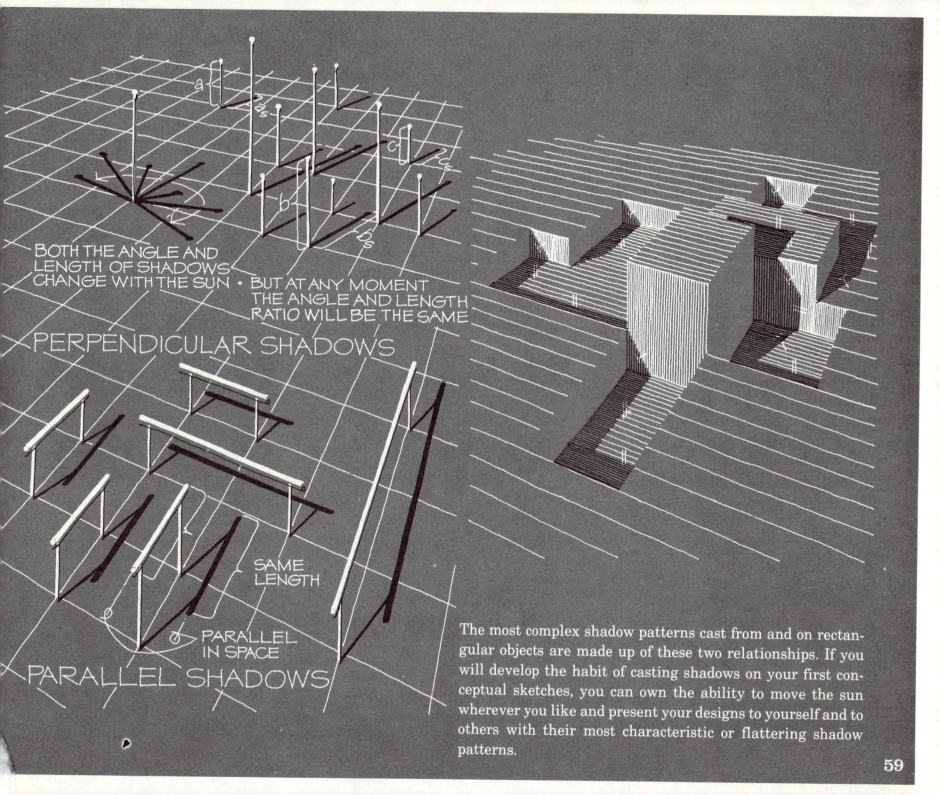

BOTH THE ANGLE AND LENGTH OF SHADOWS CHANGE WITH THE SUN · BUT AT ANY MOMENT THE ANGLE AND LENGTH RATIO WILL BE THE SAME

PERPENDICULAR SHADOWS

SAME LENGTH

PARALLEL IN SPACE

PARALLEL SHADOWS

The most complex shadow patterns cast from and on rectangular objects are made up of these two relationships. If you will develop the habit of casting shadows on your first conceptual sketches, you can own the ability to move the sun wherever you like and present your designs to yourself and to others with their most characteristic or flattering shadow patterns.

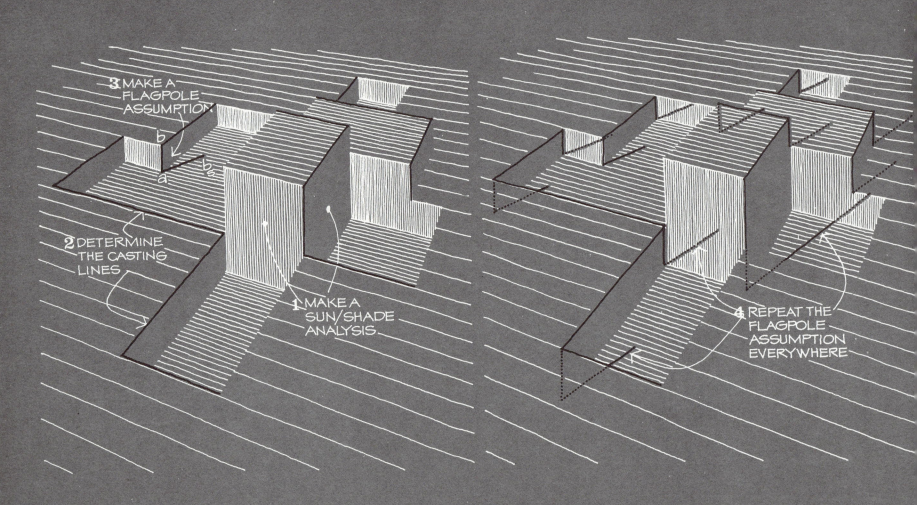

3 MAKE A FLAGPOLE ASSUMPTION

b

a

bₛ

2 DETERMINE THE CASTING LINES

1 MAKE A SUN/SHADE ANALYSIS.

4 REPEAT THE FLAGPOLE ASSUMPTION EVERYWHERE

The first step in shadow-casting is to assume the *general* direction of the sun and make a *sun/shade* analysis—determining which surfaces will be sunlit and which surfaces will be turned away from the sun, in shade.

Next, determine the *casting lines*. These are the lines which separate *sun* from *shade*, and the lines which will cast the edge of the shadow.

Next, assume the *exact* horizontal and vertical angle of the sun by assuming the direction and length of the shadow of any vertical line—like a flagpole. This may best be remembered as the *perpendicular* or *flagpole* assumption.

Then, repeat this perpendicular or flagpole assumption at all inside and outside corners, keeping the same *ratio* of flagpole length (ab) to shadow length (abs) and the same shadow direction as that of the original assumption.

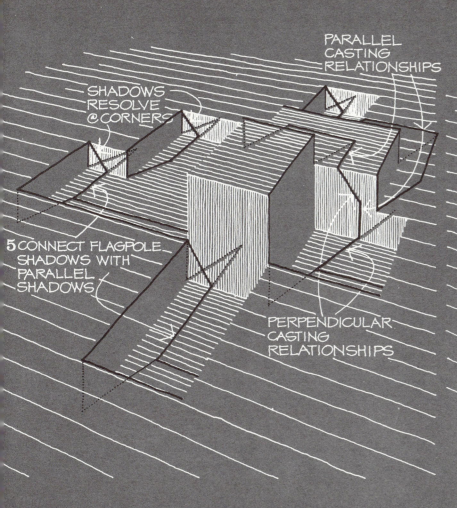

SHADOWS
RESOLVE
@CORNERS

PARALLEL
CASTING
RELATIONSHIPS

5 CONNECT FLAGPOLE
SHADOWS WITH
PARALLEL
SHADOWS

PERPENDICULAR
CASTING
RELATIONSHIPS

Next, connect all the perpendicular of flagpole shadows with *parallel* shadows, keeping the connecting shadows parallel to the portion of the casting line which is casting them. When a *parallel* shadow hits a wall the casting relationship changes— becomes perpendicular and travels up the wall at an angle, either resolving by meeting the end of the casting line, or changing again to parallel, as on a roof.

All that remains is to hatch or tone in the shadows, remembering to hatch them darker than shade. If you have cast the shadows correctly:

all the perpendicular shadows will be parallel to one another and have the same proportional length ratio to the lines which cast them;

all the parallel shadows will be parallel to one another and the same length as the lines which cast them;

no shadows will fall on surfaces which are in shade.

61

BUILDING MATERIALS

Permit me to illustrate the drawing of the various building materials with the cartoon of a building across page. Architects and authors can very easily take their work too seriously and besides, the variety of building materials which should be covered is more easily drawn in one building such as an architect would never seriously design.

In drawing the construction materials it is best to concentrate on their textural and formal character and not their color or tone. Any attempt to show a material's inherent darkness or lightness may confuse the more important aspect of light in the space or on the object.

In addition to showing a material's texture, drawing should indicate the building material unit. In paneling or siding this would mean clearly delineating the individual board or panel; in masonry the individual stone or masonry unit. I have generally found it just as meaningful and much more efficient to indicate only the bed joints or horizontal courses of brick or concrete block. This is characteristic of the way brick or block is laid and eliminates the tedious drawing of the vertical head joints which may vary with the particular bond selected.

The profile of a building material where it corners is a very effective means of showing its character. The indentation of a joint in masonry can be much more effectively shown in profile than by shadow casting in the joint. This profiling also applies to lap siding, standing seam roofs, and the top and bottom of board and batten.

Today's materials are less demanding to draw, but are often so similar in surface texture that they are difficult to invest with any character in a drawing. Aluminum, stainless steel, in fact all the metals, glass, formica, porcelain enamel, vinyl floor covering and many other modern slick, maintenance-free materials are almost impossible to make distinguishable in a simple line drawing.

Concrete presents another problem in that it can take almost any form the architect chooses, and most of these forms are difficult to represent clearly in a drawing. Exposed aggregate can be made clear in a vertical surface, but on a horizontal plane is easily confused with gravel. The imprint of rough formwork can be indicated by horizontal courses of random vertical lines as in the chimney foundation wall across page. Further subtleties in surface texture of concrete are difficult to indicate.

In drawing wood it is best to avoid great swirly patterns in the grain and be content with straight, pointy conservative patterns. Deliberately vary the spacing between lines in the wood grains.

Material indications should be economical in effort so that they make clear the textural character of the particular material without ostentatiously calling attention to themselves. The joints between different materials will be clearer if you draw (and if there actually is) a marked difference in their character.

GLASS AND WATER

Both glass and water, under most daytime lighting conditions, are primarily *reflective* materials. In spite of the fact that the rendering of reflections is extremely simple, glass and water are perhaps the most mis-rendered of architectural materials. This misrepresentation is unfortunate, and especially so for glass since it is one of modern architecture's prime materials. In addition to misleading the client, the representation of glass as either transparent or opaque misleads the designer and perverts his understanding of glass or water as architectural materials.

Looked through from an interior space, glass will be completely transparent. However, when glass is viewed from the exterior, it becomes a mirror for its surroundings because it is a highly polished membrane separating a relatively dark interior volume from a relatively bright exterior.

The reflection of everything which lies outside a vertical glass window will appear to have been pulled back perpendicularly through the glass to a position which is the same distance *behind* the glass as it actually is in front of the glass. Reflections in a horizontal pool of water appear similarly except that, instead of being pulled horizontally through the glass toward the vanishing point, they appear to have been pulled vertically the same distance *below* the surface of the water as they actually are above it. Regardless of what drawing technique you are using, I have found that reflections help establish the plane of the reflective surface if you render glass reflections with straight vertical tones of lines and water reflections with wiggly horizontal tones of lines.

It is useful to divide the reflections in glass into two realms. The first realm is that between the viewer and the glass, and includes everything that actually appears in the perspective. This realm should be reflected as having the same tonal range as it actually has. The second realm is everything that lies behind the viewer and does not appear in the perspective *except* as reflections in the glass. This second realm is best delineated as receding, progressively lighter layers of space— buildings, trees, mountains—rendered as vertical tones of lines. Above the reflections of this second realm, beginning a little above eye level, the sky behind the viewer will be reflected, and this sky reflection will normally be the brightest part of the reflections in the glass. In black and white drawings this sky reflection should be left white; in colored drawings like the sepia print on page 53, this sky reflection should be tinted a light blue and might have cloud reflections in it.

Reflectivity is the most characteristic and exciting quality of glass and water as exterior architectural materials. The reflections in glass double the apparent thickness of walls by reflecting the jamb or head of an opening. Both glass and water can respond to a beautiful natural environment or distinguished older buildings by reflecting them in a way no other material can, and your designs and the drawings with which you represent them should reflect this understanding.

CONTENTS AND CONTEXT

In addition to drawing architecture, an architect must master the drawing of a certain amount of "stuff" with which to surround and fill his architecture. This "stuff" is really rather limited in scope: figures, furniture, trees and planting, and automobiles. We should be grateful for this limited demand on our drawing ability. Compared to that of a magazine illustrator or a cartoonist our graphic vocabulary is rudimentary.

In spite of the limited scope of the contents and context, they are very important to any architectural drawing. This entourage can demonstrate the scale of the space, indicate its use, and in doing so, humanize the drawing. Care, however, must be taken that the "stuff" never overpowers the architecture. It should be reduced to simple graphic conventions, remaining as realistic as possible, but never over-rendered.

HUMANIZING THE DRAWING

To demonstrate the humanizing of a drawing, let's take a drawing with which you should be quite familiar by now and fill it with stuff. The drawing across page is perhaps overfull but several rules have been carefully followed:

1. Never obscure important, space-defining intersections, such as intersections of ceiling and wall, or floor and wall.
2. Use simple outlines and a minimum of detail in drawing the figures, furniture, and plants.

3. Do not make the figures overactive in posture, and always collect them into groups.

This is an appropriate place to talk about a very important means of representing the third or depth dimension in perspective drawing: "lapping" or stacking up objects in space so that they convey a sense of depth by dividing a depth into smaller increments. This technique was well-known to the cubists: witness a Braque still life. Psychologists have shown that this division of a given depth into a number of pieces actually increases the illusion of depth.

Given this means of demonstrating depth, any adjustments of line weight or tone as an indication of depth become insignificant by comparison. The articulation of space into receding layers by the placement of objects in the space is one of the real values of the entourage or stuff we have been talking about. In the drawing across page you can see this lapping of objects. The greatest number of laps is where the space is deepest. This deepest series of laps is: coffee table, woman's leg, sofa, woman, man, sliding door, man, man, wall, building in distance, trees, foothills and mountains.

In succeeding pages the drawing of figures, furniture, plants and automobiles will be dealt with separately. It is worthwhile to master their delineation. Be careful not to make the mistake of shifting the emphasis from the architecture to the contents or the context. This will be dealt with later under "Emphasis."

FIGURES

Architectural drawings should include the human figure. Figures give scale to the spaces in the drawing. By their posture, disposition, number, and dress they help to indicate the use of the space. Their placement on upper or lower levels can indicate floor levels and spaces which are otherwise difficult to delineate. But the most important reason for the inclusion of figures in architectural drawings is that architecture exists only to serve people and must relate to the size of the human figure. By keeping figures in our drawings, we will be reminded of this and, hopefully, will design seats, walls, windows, and doors which better accept the human figure.

The easiest way to draw figures, I have found, is to draw the head at eye level (a lower level of about four feet if the figure is seated) and proceed downward, using the general geometric outline shown on the opposite page. The size of the head may then have to be readjusted to be proportioned to the body which develops.

Except at stiff attention, the human figure is seldom symmetrical. We tend to stand with our weight disposed unevenly on our legs and our arms are normally positioned differently. So, below the head, draw the shoulder slope, the elbow "bulges" (which occur unless the arms are held stiffly down), and the legs asymmetrically to indicate an uneven stance.

Seated figures will relate better to table and chair if you place the elbows on the table. Later, if you wish, they may be discreetly removed and hands placed in the lap, but the figure's head, shoulders, and seat can be better established with elbows on the table. Several typical seated postures should be mastered — legs crossed, ankles crossed, elbow or arm over seat back, arm on chair arm or figure braced by hand on seat. Certain gestures and head angles can help relate a group of figures and make clear who is talking and who is listening. Figures are easier to draw if you avoid the profile of either the head or body. The profile is a very active line and calls too much attention to the figure.

The figures should be doing something in the space — not just standing stiffly alone. Neither should they be running, jumping, or moving actively lest they call too much attention to themselves. They should be using the space by conversing, sitting, viewing, or walking. It is always better to draw figures in clusters, relating to one another. Whenever possible they should also relate to the architecture by sitting on it, leaning against it, or looking through it. If there are no places in your space to sit, lean, look through, or stand pleasantly, then perhaps it isn't a very human space.

Despite the importance of figures in architectural drawings they should remain secondary to the architecture. Their placement should be such that they do not obscure important space-defining intersections. And they should be drawn with an absolute minimum of detail. One way of assuring this is to draw them as simple ghostlike outlines. In this form they will fulfill all the reasons for their inclusion without preempting the architecture.

TREES AND GROUND COVERS IN PLAN

Architectural plans have traditionally included the area around the building and an indication of the design of this area: the paved areas, the planted areas, trees and ground cover. Once this peripheral area was designed exclusively to reinforce the geometry of the building. Today more of our buildings occupy urban sites and the space surrounding the building, if any, is more properly seen as a transition space which should relate the geometry and circulation pattern of the building to the surrounding site context.

In addition to communicating the design of the area surrounding the building, the trees, shrubs and paving help give scale and embellish the plan visually as a drawing.

There are many ways to indicate plan entourage; across page you see a sample of some of them. The tree indications range from rather specific ones to very abstract ones. The paving patterns are all very specific. Depending on the degree of concern you have for the detail of landscaping, or whether you rely on consultants for this, you may choose to represent landscaping in specific detail or in generalized abstractions. The very best way is to have a knowledge of the landscape materials reasonable to the design climate and draw them so that they communicate to you and to others the characteristics that are theirs.

There are many other conventional entourage indications, and with a little thought these can be varied and new ones invented interminably. The important thing is to learn to draw a few of them and learn how long the various techniques take so that in a time-pinch you can select the ones which give the best effect for the least effort.

Another important consideration is to choose entourage which is consistent with your architectural plan in detail and realism so that the entourage always complements the architecture without overpowering or detracting from it.

It may be helpful to show the construction of one of the basic tree forms in plan.

Great numbers of trees at small scale merit a simpler indication than any across page.

A very useful continuous stroke that is worth mastering is the "*Squarus Leafila Trailiatum.*"

And finally two oft-confused ornamental shrubs: the "*Pinwheelus Clockwiseum*" and the "*Pinwheelus Counterclockwiseum.*"

TREES AND GROUND COVERS IN PERSPECTIVE

The unlikely landscape on the next page is a composite of trees and ground textures in perspective or elevation. The same considerations apply here as did in plan. Remember that the entourage in a drawing, and in reality, should act as a foil for the building, complementing and enhancing the architecture.

There are two techniques in the drawing of entourage. One is realistic, in which the forms are built up of tiny individual geometric units indicating leaves. The other is more abstract in that the character of the units is only suggested by the character of the outline of the total form. The two trees in the upper left-hand corner are the best examples of these two approaches.

Trees in perspective can and should have a more specific character than in plan. The branching habit, leaf form, and overall size and shape of the tree should be as realistic as your knowledge and design effort permit. I hope you can distinguish an oak, a palm, an olive and some evergreens across page. That pretty well stretches my specific tree vocabulary, largely because I only recently have attached any importance to the ability to draw specific trees. I well remember that for years the architectural profession rode along on the few which Ted Kautzky drew in *Pencil Broadsides*. His birch trees were delineated in front of buildings sited where no birch ever grew.

You may experiment with casting shadows on the ground from the entourage, but generally I have found it to be extremely complex and time-consuming for the contribution it makes. Let only the architecture cast shadows on itself and on the ground. The sun will then help indicate what it is that is important in your drawing and differentiate it from a landscape painting.

One of the most useful strokes I have found in rough sketching trees, and particularly masses of trees or planting, is what could be called the "umbrella" stroke, having a rather simple convex form on top and a rather complex concave conformation below.

Trees in the near foreground can be useful to frame a perspective and their undersides a convenient place to stop the tone or blue of a sky.

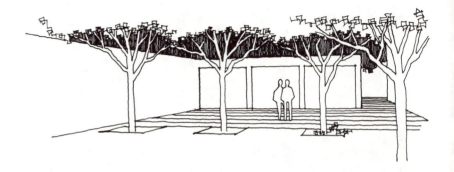

This happens to be an excellent graphic illustration of the potential trees have as architectural, space-defining elements.

AUTOMOBILES

Automobiles are part of the necessary entourage which surrounds and fills architecture. There are two approaches to drawing cars. One is to draw carefully an exact model of a particular car, a 1966 Ford Mustang or a Volkswagen Microbus. The other approach is to draw a completely characterless car — a "car" car — simple, understated, having no special features. Both these approaches are valid, since they do essentially the same thing. They represent the object without competing with the architecture — the exact models because they are familiar, and thus not a design element, and the characterless forms because they make no design statement.

Both approaches avoid the trap into which the beginning architectural designer invariably falls: the attempt to *design* everything in sight. The cars can become competing design statements which overpower the architecture. Architects will never, and should never, have the opportunity or responsibility for designing the whole world, in spite of all you may hear about "total environment." Have the wisdom to limit your design time and abilities to that which is your direct responsibility — the building. You must, however, know well and be able to draw the contemporary industrial products which relate to architecture.

Keep figures next to automobiles as you draw them. An automobile's relation to the human figure is one of the surest ways to draw an automobile correctly. Since all automobiles are designed to relate to the human figure, the placement of a figure next to an automobile will immediately show whether an automobile is too low, too high, too large, or too small.

Almost all of today's cars are low enough to see over and thus will appear entirely below eye level. In drawing an automobile, first draw a rectangular box, as shown across page. With only slight angles and batters this will become a respectable car form. To draw a particular model will take more work and require an advertisement or brochure at hand. You may want to draw a particular model when only one car is required in the drawing, but when many cars are indicated, I have found it wiser to be content to draw a characterless "car" car.

The great masses of parking which surround many contemporary buildings and which must be included in the drawing, if we are to render honestly, can be delineated by indicating the profile of their tops and drawing no detail at all.

Automobiles are anathema to most modern architects. They bury them, plant trees over them and above all keep them far away from their precious buildings. This attitude is reflected in their drawings. Automobiles are seldom seen in architectural drawings. This attitude has always puzzled me since most of our architecture is first seen from automobiles. The experience of arrival begins as a passenger in an automobile and thus our experience of architecture is inseparable from it. Beyond this the automobile is perhaps the strongest symbol of our affluent independence and mobility — our individual freedom.

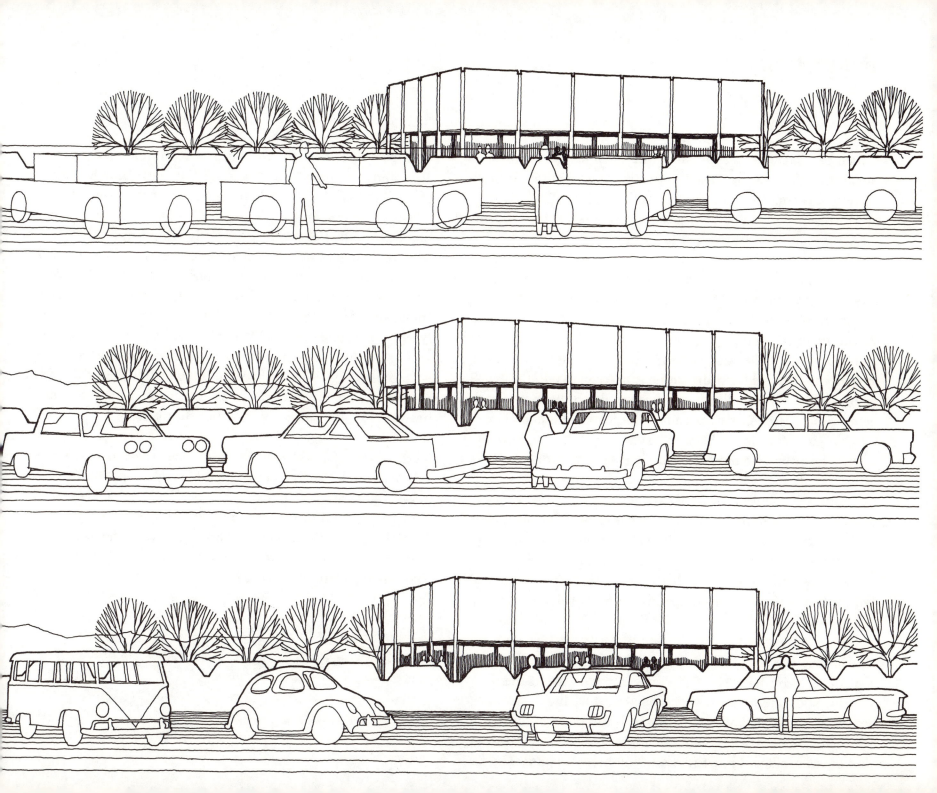

FURNITURE

Much of what was just said about automobiles also applies to furniture. The two approaches are the same. One is to draw exactly a particular chair, sofa, or table — a Barcelona chair or a Matthson table. The alternate approach is to draw a completely characterless article of furniture.

With furniture there is more reason to know and be able to draw specific pieces of furniture. Architects are much more likely to be asked to choose a client's furniture than to choose his automobile. And so you should be prepared by a thorough knowledge of well-designed furniture. Many architects have contributed classic furniture designs, particularly to the Knoll and Herman Miller collections. Mies van der Rohe, Eero Saarinen, Marcel Breuer, Alvar Aalto, Charles Eames and George Nelson are a few of the better known architects who have designed furniture. Some of their designs appear across page.

As with automobiles, avoid designing the furniture yourself, unless you are prepared to master a whole new field of design. In any case do not design, draw or choose furniture which upstages the architecture. The furniture designed by the architects above is admirable in this respect. It is all understated and conservative, never competing with its surroundings for attention.

Furniture, particularly foreground furniture, is often drawn out of scale by beginners. The surest way to avoid this is to draw a standing figure with his head eyeball high (see "Perspective" page 11) and his feet next to the piece of furniture. With this done it will be almost impossible to draw furniture out of scale, since it must relate to the human figure. The fig-ures may always be erased later having fulfilled their purpose of keeping the furniture in scale. If you have time and as you develop the skill, you should place figures on or in the furniture.

Simple characterless furniture is fairly easy to draw, if you stick with rectangular shapes. Some furniture groupings, however, particularly a dining table and chairs, become a welter of legs and cross braces. There is no very good way to fake such a thing, and there is nothing for it but to construct it as accurately as possible and draw it. Don't be afraid to cover up furniture with other furniture in a perspective. This foreshortening and stacking up of objects in space can help the illusion of the third dimension, even if it means wasting some of your background drawing by obscuring it with other furniture.

This may be the best place to make one other point. Horizontal, plan circles such as circular tables or lamps, bowls or recessed lights are not tipped in perspective. The tendency is to tip them up toward the viewer in what is closer to a plan view or make them distortedly respond to one of the perspective axes. They do actually respond to perspective even when you draw them horizontal and flat.

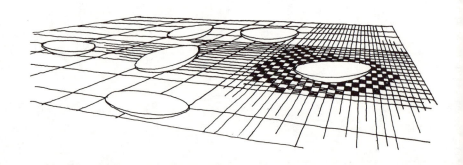

EFFICIENCY AND WISDOM IN DRAWING

Time is perhaps our only absolutely limited individual resource. This limitation applies just as surely to drawing and architecture as to anything else. The repeated meeting of deadlines in architectural education and architectural practice is rather poignant in its parallel to mortality. Any deadline must be accepted as a very real determinant in drawing or design. The question can never be, "How well can I draw it?" but, "How well can I draw it or design it within the available time?"

The first thing a student of drawing must realize is that drawing demands vast amounts of time. The areas of a finished pen and ink rendering which look as if they took hours and hours and near-infinite patience *did* take hours and hours and near-infinite patience. The first "plateau" in architectural drawing is reached when the student makes a time commitment to drawing sufficient to carefully render a presentation completely, with time at the end to seek criticism and make minor corrections and adjustments in response to criticism. At that moment he realizes how much time it takes, but he also knows that it is possible to devote that much time, even enthusiastically, and hopefully he knows the satisfaction that can come from the successful completion of a difficult task which demands both mind and hand.

Speed in drawing, as in most other things, comes from a thorough mastery of fundamentals. A miler does not attempt to beat four minutes his first time out. First it is necessary to learn *how* to run. Until this is accomplished any attempt at great speed is unsuccessful and may even be damaging. In drawing, speed will come with the mastery of certain graphic conventions and the knowledge and correct choice of these conven-

tions in relation to the time they take. You will simply learn to draw faster by drawing more.

In architectural practice the solution to the deadline for client presentation seems to lie in the development of a rough sketching technique which looks professional and actually uses process-study-design-means drawings as presentation drawings. If you can develop such a sketching technique I think you will find it eagerly accepted by clients. They will feel a greater sense of participation in the process of the design of the building, which is in every way desirable, and you will not need to risk, and often waste, great amounts of time in laboriously rendered presentations. You can rather use that time to make stacks of rough studies and refinements, any one of which will be worthy of showing to the client.

I can suggest a few tactics which I have found useful in managing the available time to make any drawing:

Be conservative in your choice of techniques and indications. Avoid unpredictable graphic experiments and untried shortcuts. They often take much more time than they save;

Choose techniques and indications which quickly become respectably or acceptably complete, but accept continuous balanced improvement as suggested later in DRAWING AS AN INVESTMENT HIERARCHY;

Develop a continuously updated awareness, as you make the drawings, of the balance of the entire presentation and an extended ranked list of "what I may not need to draw."

THE OVERLAY

Architects normally draw on transparent paper. The original reason for the transparency of the paper probably had to do with multiple reproductions from transparent originals on light-sensitive paper — blueprinting. Drawing on transparent paper has, for me, a much more important potential for architectural design. This potential is the possibility of overlaying drawings and refining them in a continuing process. This use of the overlay is employed by most architects as a habitual part of their design method.

Refinement by overlay has two uses, similar but different in purpose. The most important use is the refinement of the design of the building; the continually improved reshaping of the plan, the proportioning of the spaces, and then the refinement of the window openings, entrances and other details. The similar, secondary use of refinement by overlay is the refinement of drawing.

These two kinds of refinement often occur simultaneously. As the design progresses toward some optimum, so does the drawing. Both the refinement processes are affected by similar determinants. The chief of these determinants is the available budget of time and money, yours and your client's.

Overlaying should continue as long as uninvestigated design options exist or until further options are ruled out by confident intellectual decisions. Time often preempts both these logical conclusions to the overlaying, refining process. Further refinement in drawing is unjustified beyond this point where all design decisions have been made, except when a very formal presentation is indicated or when it is done just for the joy of drawing it up "first class."

Important to the technique of overlaying is the idea that no single drawing is important except in its relation to the one below and the one above as a link in a developing process. The cheapest possible paper and its conspicuous consumption encourage the technique. In addition to its direct usefulness, the technique is symbolic of the developmental process of design, and even of the concept of culture.

In reference to this overlaying technique the phrase "a thin design" has particular significance. It means that there was no thickness of development overlays — that instead of being twenty or thirty overlays thick, the design is just as thin as the one piece of paper on which it now appears.

I have always puzzled over the tenacity with which teachers cling to opaque paper and illustration boards instead of letting their students benefit from the advantages of transparent paper, not the least of which is this idea of drawings being only one stage in a process.

The series which follows demonstrates one way such an overlay series might progress. The first overlay on buff tracing paper might be the kind a designer would make for himself. Many designers hang their sketches up around them and "live" with them—spend long periods of time just looking at them, attending to what the drawings can tell them. Drawn representations can hold more complex interrelated information than we could possibly carry in our mind and see holistically. So at some point in any design process, the design concept is transferred to the drawings and exists *in the drawings* much more completely and complexly than in the designer's mind.

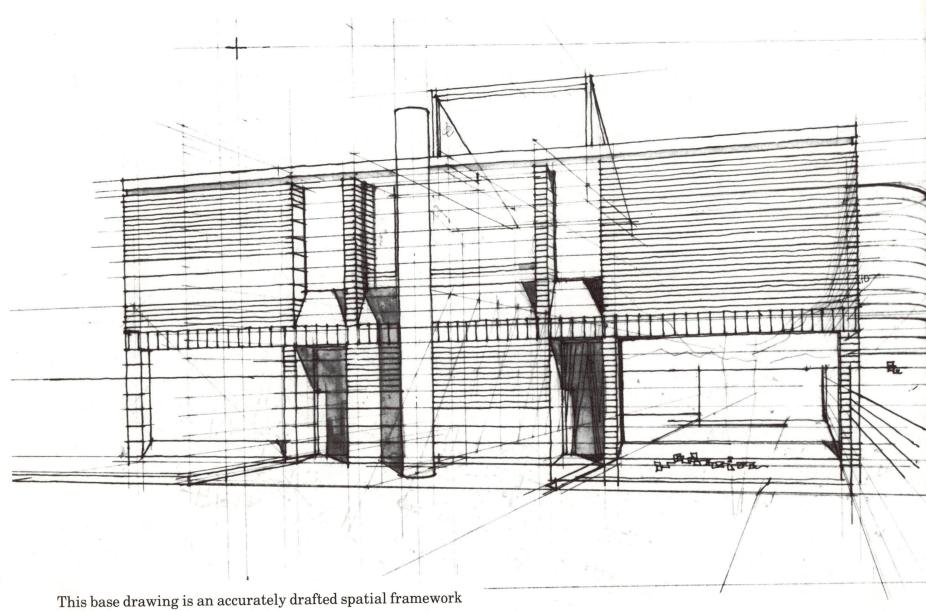

This base drawing is an accurately drafted spatial framework using the perspective method proposed earlier. If you plan to invest any time in studying or presenting a design, this step is an absolutely necessary investment. Once made, you can confidently use the framework as an underlay for freehand studies and presentations.

The first few times you make one of these, the process will seem tedious and confusing, but repetitive use of the method will imprint it to the point where you can make a base drawing in less than an hour.

Most architects draw on buff tracing paper and this overlay is the kind of first overlay I make for myself. All the elements are tested briefly in rough form. Shadows, landscaping, glass reflections and the beginnings of other material indications are all there. From this very quick sketch I now know the potential of both the design and the drawing.

Further studies of the design depend on opportunities I see for improvement and are potentially infinite. Further refinement of the drawing, however, will wait until it is necessary to communicate to someone else in a more formal way.

Most architects draw on buff tracing paper and this overlay is the kind of first overlay I make for myself. All the elements are tested briefly in rough form. Shadows, landscaping, glass reflections and the beginnings of other material indications are all there. From this very quick sketch I now know the potential of both the design and the drawing.

Further studies of the design depend on opportunities I see for improvement and are potentially infinite. Further refinement of the drawing, however, will wait until it is necessary to communicate to someone else in a more formal way.

This overlay demonstrates the final potential of this way of drawing on buff tracing paper. It was made with a fountain pen, gray marker and three Prismacolor pencils. As a one-of-a-kind original which retains that kind of freshness, it is probably good enough for clients whom you don't need to impress with formality.

For reproduction or more formal communication, a different technique and a great deal more time is required. If you can develop your second, rough overlay technique to the point where they are acceptable client communications, you will save yourself vast amounts of non-design time.

This overlay demonstrates the final potential of this way of drawing on buff tracing paper. It was made with a fountain pen, gray marker and three Prismacolor pencils. As a one-of-a-kind original which retains that kind of freshness, it is probably good enough for clients whom you don't need to impress with formality.

For reproduction or more formal communication, a different technique and a great deal more time is required. If you can develop your second, rough overlay technique to the point where they are acceptable client communications, you will save yourself vast amounts of non-design time.

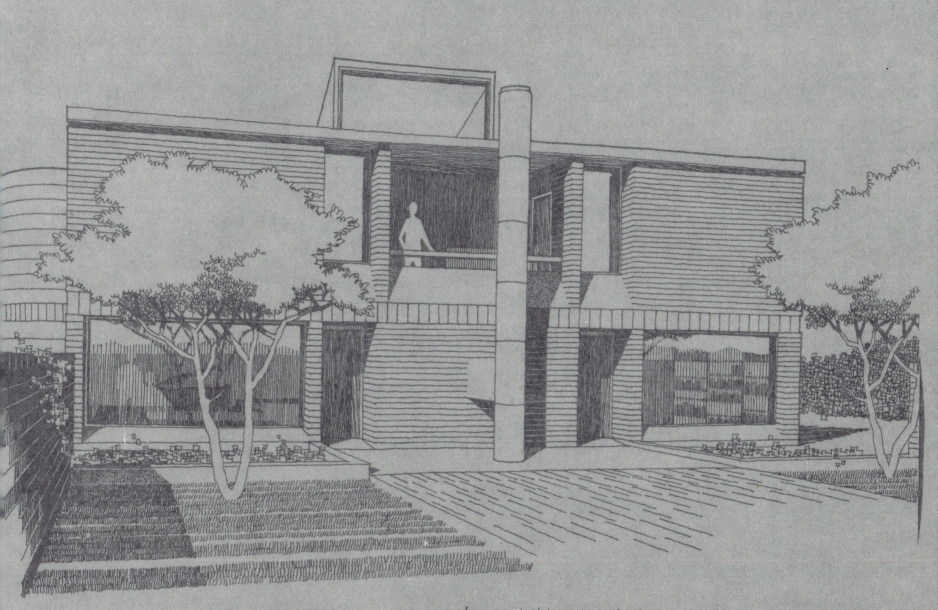

This last overlay represents a major investment in time and would probably be necessary for publication or some sort of rather formal presentation. It also is only one form such a final overlay might take.

Formal presentations should always be only one final overlay of drawings you have already made in the normal course of the design process.

This last overlay represents a major investment in time and would probably only be necessary for publication or some sort of rather formal presentation. It also is only one form such a final overlay might take.

Formal presentations should always be only one final overlay of drawings you have already made in the normal course of the design process.

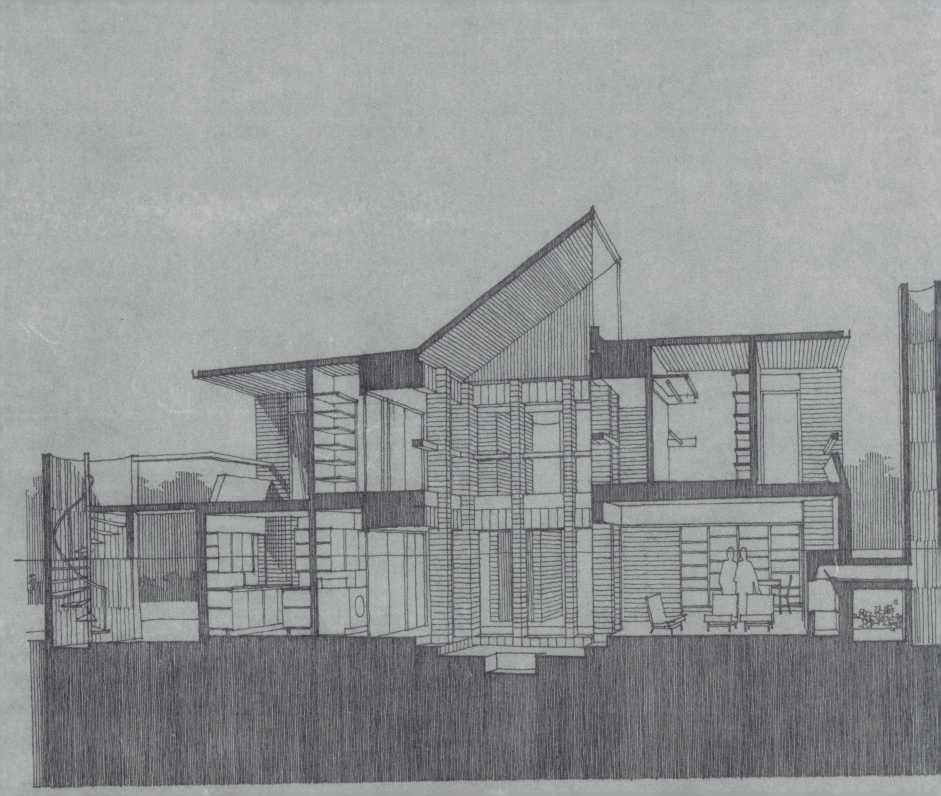

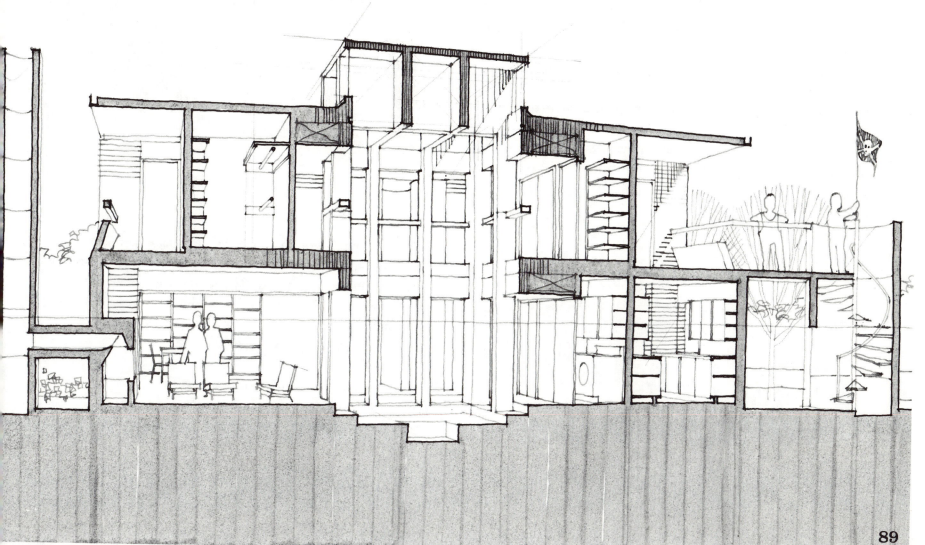

EMPHASIS

In architectural drawing the emphasis should be on the architecture. By "architecture" I would accept Christian Norberg-Schulz's definition of the elements of architecture as being mass, space, and surface, — surfaces being mass-boundary or space-boundary. This placement of emphasis on the architecture seems obvious, yet I have seen exteriors drawn like landscapes and interiors drawn like furniture showrooms.

This misplacement of emphasis can be demonstrated as follows:

In the left-hand sketch below the emphasis is on the non-architectural object in the space. In the right-hand sketch the emphasis is correctly on the architectural space and the space-bounding surface.

In the left-hand sketch above the emphasis is on the surrounding landscape. In the sketch on the right the emphasis is more correctly on the architectural mass and the mass-bounding surfaces as revealed in sunlight. I would refer you to the drawings of Wright and Neutra as beautiful examples of correctly placed emphasis in architectural drawing.

Another case of misplaced emphasis is the case of the emphasis on a virtuoso drawing technique. Just as architecture is not really a performing art, even less should architectural drawing be a vehicle for the display of technique. The drawings must communicate the quality of the architecture without competing for the attention of the viewer. The comment of the viewer should be, "This is a beautiful building," or "a powerful space" and only as an afterthought ". . . and very clearly delineated."

Architectural students often mistakenly believe that excellence in architectural drawing consists of being able to draw certain foreground entourage skillfully. The surest sign of a thin architectural design is the preempting of the architecture by meaningless cliché entourage in drawing, and in exactly the same way in real buildings. A palm tree through the roof or the latest sunscreen pasted on the facade are two of a host of painfully clear visual deodorants.

Their counterparts in drawing are "cute" foreground figures or an over-rendered car, or tree at center stage. I have found these often are put in in the final stage of presentation as an attempt to perk up a bland drawing. The problem may be that the drawing is a correct drawing of a bland design.

The whole concept in drawing, and in design, of "adding a little punch," or "popping it out," which you have all heard, is very disturbing to me. The quality of architecture, if there is any, is integral and of long standing in the design process, and is little affected by any last minute seasoning.

If it is a building that you are drawing, then draw it, for yourself and for others, as a work of architecture. Always communicate your designs to yourself and to others from the earliest drawing in all possible honesty. Architectural drawing cannot be allowed the freedom of abstraction. It must be completely representational or it is worthless, or at best, misleading.

This demand for representational honesty applies to perspectives, elevations, sections and floor plans and even to the more abstract realm discussed in "Other Graphic Means." The point here is that the drawings should be representational of architectural ideas: if a stone wall is represented then the drawing should look as much like a stone wall as possible; if the building will be built in a cluttered urban context then that should be represented.

The incorrect alternative to this is a misplaced emphasis on some sort of grand sheet compositional scheme as in Beaux Arts presentations where the importance of the two-dimensional graphic composition often completely overwhelmed the communication of architectural ideas.

An example of this is the rendering of elevations as black and white patterns of black windows and white walls as if the walls really were white illustration board and the windows were white illustration board painted with India ink. An architectural drawing which takes great amounts of time to present a building in this way without a more realistic representation of materials or tactile quality or sunlight and shadow is in my view worthless. The emphasis is not on architecture but on cardboard and ink.

Correctly placed emphasis can contribute to your drawing efficiency. Speed in drawing is not a matter of last minute graphic inspirations or frenetic hand speed; it is rather the cool management of a disciplined process and includes knowing what *not* to draw. Careful control of the architectural emphasis of a drawing will keep your design attention where it should be and coincidentally save a great deal of your time.

LETTERING

Architects have traditionally been good letterers. Lettering is demanded on working drawings and on more detailed preliminaries, particularly plans. Recently the advent of the rub-on, stick-on, buy-'em-by-the-sheet letters has given many architects, and particularly students, the idea that a knowledge of and skill in calligraphy are no longer important.

Perhaps I'm old fashioned, or Scotch enough to be irritated at having drawers full of Q's, X's, and Z's left over, but lettering is one of those quaint old skills like tying a bow tie that isn't so complex that we need surrender it to the machine. Some night, after all the stores are closed, you may run out of E's — and then what will you do? Misspell the word? Or change to lower case? I have seen students do both.

Even if we are affluent enough to buy all our letters so that we *never* have to letter, we will still be required to place lettering on our buildings; and the design and placement of a sign or text requires a knowledge and appreciation of the form, character and spacing of letters that cannot be purchased for the price of a sticky sheet of acetate.

Our alphabets have had the benefit of centuries of refinement. It is very difficult to improve on the various lettering styles now in use. There are many excellent reference collections of alphabets and type faces and one of these should be a part of your library. Spend your time learning and selecting the available lettering styles rather than trying to design your own.

The shaded-stroke letter, in which there are two definitely different widths of stroke, should be mastered so that you know which strokes of an A, U, M, N, W, etc., are fat and which are skinny. It is very disturbing when the position of the shaded stroke is changed. A test of an understanding of lettering form is to be able to develop an entirely consistent alphabet after being given only the M and the R.

All the alphabets across page were lettered freehand except the third one and the numbers at the bottom, which were traced. If an alphabet has enough character and each letter has a consistent form, the lettering will look good even if freehand.

It is perhaps easier to make a very stylish lettering look consistent. The next to the last alphabet is one of the more stylish. I learned it from Santry Fuller. The way each stroke begins and ends is very important and recalls the serif of a Roman letter. The alphabet thus has enough character to make even early attempts at lettering hold together and appear consistent.

I find the completely plain alphabets like the fifth one to be the most difficult to letter well and at the same time perhaps the best for architectural drawing. They are content to just lie there communicating without making a design or style statement.

ABCDEFGHIJKLMNOPQRST
UVWXYZ   1234567890

ABCDEFGHIJIKLMNOPQRSTUVWXYZ

ABCDEFGHIJKLMNOPQRSTUVWXYZ

ABCDEFGHIJKLMNOPQRSTUVW SECTION ELEVATION

ABCDEFGHIJKLMNOPQRSTUVWXYZ PERSPECTIVE PLAN

abcdefghijklmnopqrstuvwxyz bedroom concourse

ABCDEFGHIJKLMNOPQRSTUVWXYZ FAMILY ROOM

ABCDEFGHIJKLMNOPQRSTUVWXYZ SANCTUARY NARTHEX

1234567890 *Architect*

93

TAPES AND TEMPLATES

Learning to draw can be thought of as the making of perceptual tapes which are stored away in the learner's memory bank. What appears as incredibly efficient drawing ability is simply the replaying of such perceptual tapes developed long ago and stored for convenient retrieval. The tapes monitor and control the feedback loop which links the eye and hand. This kind of continuously adjusted control is called *cybernetics* and in drawing is dependent on having a control loop or perceptual *template* of the tree, figure or chair in your stored experience. Learning to draw is much more accurately thought of as the training of your *perception* rather than your hand, for only your trained perception can control your hand.

Fortunately, architects only need to master the drawing of a very limited slice of the visual world, as introduced under CONTENTS AND CONTEXT, page 66, and much of what we need to draw can be reduced to perceptual templates. These templates need to come in several scales, just like the familiar green toilet templates distributed by American-Standard. The scales are at once differentiated by their distance and their detail or the time they take to draw. As an example of this scale/time variation, your tree-template collection should include a 10 second tree, a 5 minute tree and a 30 minute tree; and these should roughly correspond to your 500 yard (away) tree, your 30 yard tree and your 12 foot tree.

The most valuable templates are those which are time-flexible so that they become visually respectable very quickly, but can accept and continue to benefit from further attention if the time becomes available. If you develop the habit of looking at architectural drawings as the graphic records of a series of acts and try to discover what was done first, second and third and then practice duplicating that process, you will soon own a bulging bag of perceptual tapes or templates. One of the best collections of such templates is *A Graphic Vocabulary for Architectural Presentation* by Tim White, who teaches with me at the University of Arizona. The direct tracing of figures, trees and furniture is a reasonable way to begin your own collection.

This may sound like I am suggesting the removal of all the creativity from drawing, but creativity in architectural drawing does not consist of continually inventing new ways of drawing the man-made environment. First of all your creativity should largely be reserved for the architecture. If you make an architectural drawing to show how well you can draw you misunderstand and are misusing drawing. Creativity in drawing should be reserved for choosing the right drawings at the right time to study and communicate your designs.

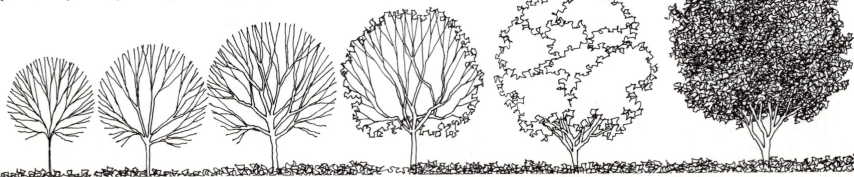

DRAWING AS AN INVESTMENT HIERARCHY

Efficiency in drawing is further served by subdividing the total visual interest of a drawing into categories which can be added in a managed progression beginning with the most efficient interest categories. The drawing process then has the "upfront" hierarchy of newspaper articles which are written without the knowledge of how much space they will be given so that they can be cut off anywhere after the first paragraph and still be essentially complete.

Such a hierarchial categorization is impossible to accomplish with the traditional pure media-classified techniques, since in them the various categories are virtually inseparable and any incompleteness in the drawing is painfully apparent. The LINE AND TONE technique discussed earlier on page 44, however, is quite easily separable into the following *investment hierarchy* of visual interest categories:

SPATIAL INTEREST—*promised kinesthetic interest—the anticipated experience of a variety of spaces and vistas only partially revealed which will become available as we move through the space.*

FIGURAL INTEREST—*traditionally ornamental—the interest we find in perceiving irregular sinuous lines or complexly related patterns.*

TONAL INTEREST—*the full white to black range of light— sunlight, shadow and shade.*

TEXTURAL INTEREST—*anticipated tactile interest—the indication of what certain surfaces will feel like.*

If the first rough sketches of a design promise an interesting space, you may decide to begin a series of changes and refinements which will improve the space and the drawings which represent it. At this point, it is always worth investing in an accurate, drafted spatial structure. To continue investing time in an inaccurate representative drawing is foolish.

This drawing would be a drafted overlay of a selected freehand sketch. It provides an accurate spatial structure following the perspective method described earlier, corrects significant errors in the rough freehand sketch, and makes all further overlays essentially accurate. A drafted framework such as this takes no more than an hour and is a solid investment in that it need only be done once.

SPATIAL AND FIGURAL INTEREST. This profiled open line drawing which finalizes spatial and figural interest is the first stage goal of all LINE AND TONE drawings. It is very much like the simple line drawings in children's coloring books, but everything is spatially defined and it is a very unequivocal, committed drawing. The drawing is an acceptable representation of an environment because the edges represented in line drawings carry most of the perceived information about our environment.

Spatial and figural interest in drawing are tightly interrelated. The number of hidden spaces and spatial layers or laps should be maximized and the figurally interesting objects should demonstrate the space (like the tree or the seated figure) without hiding space-defining intersections. The drawing is essentially complete but the efficiency of the hierarchy has been maintained by stopping short of the two most time-consuming interest categories.

SPATIAL AND FIGURAL INTEREST. This profiled open line drawing which finalizes spatial and figural interest is the first stage goal of all LINE AND TONE drawings. It is very much like the simple line drawings in children's coloring books, but everything is spatially defined and it is a very unequivocal, committed drawing. The drawing is an acceptable representation of an environment because the edges represented in line drawings carry most of the perceived information about our environment.

Spatial and figural interest in drawing are tightly interrelated. The number of hidden spaces and spatial layers or laps should be maximized and the figurally interesting objects should demonstrate the space (like the tree or the seated figure) without hiding space-defining intersections. The drawing is essentially complete but the efficiency of the hierarchy has been maintained by stopping short of the two most time-consuming interest categories.

TONAL INTEREST. The two remaining interest categories are both very time consuming. Tonal interest should be added next because its main source, *light,* is not as arbitrary as textural interest's chief source, materials; and because tonal interest lends itself to various technological shortcuts.

Diazo process prints, drawing on middletone, mounting a tracing paper drawing on black board and coloring on the back with white (as simulated in reverse here) or mounting white cutouts behind are some of the short cuts.

TEXTURAL INTEREST. This is the last category to be added in the investment hierarchy because it is the most time-consuming and does not lend itself to the shortcuts available to tonal interest. This category is also, perhaps, the most changeable (in its material choices) of the categories. Textures should first be applied to the space-bounding architectural surfaces beginning with the floor.

The hierarchy suggested here sounds like a very mechanical inhuman way of making a drawing and I am not advocating it as the best way of drawing. It is, however, the most efficient way to draw and any designer should know about it for those times when his efficiency is paramount.

TEXTURAL INTEREST. This is the last category to be added in the investment hierarchy because it is the most time-consuming and does not lend itself to the shortcuts available to tonal interest. This category is also, perhaps, the most changeable (in its material choices) of the categories. Textures should first be applied to the space-bounding architectural surfaces beginning with the floor.

The hierarchy suggested here sounds like a very mechanical inhuman way of making a drawing and I am not advocating it as the best way of drawing. It is, however, the *most efficient* way to draw and any designer should know about it for those times when his efficiency is paramount.

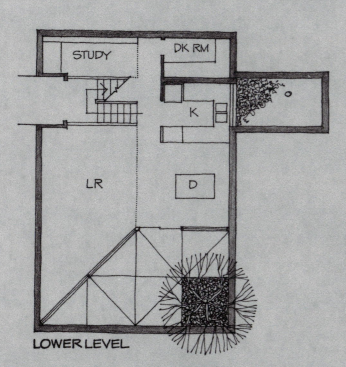

LOWER LEVEL

STUDY

DK RM

K

LR

D

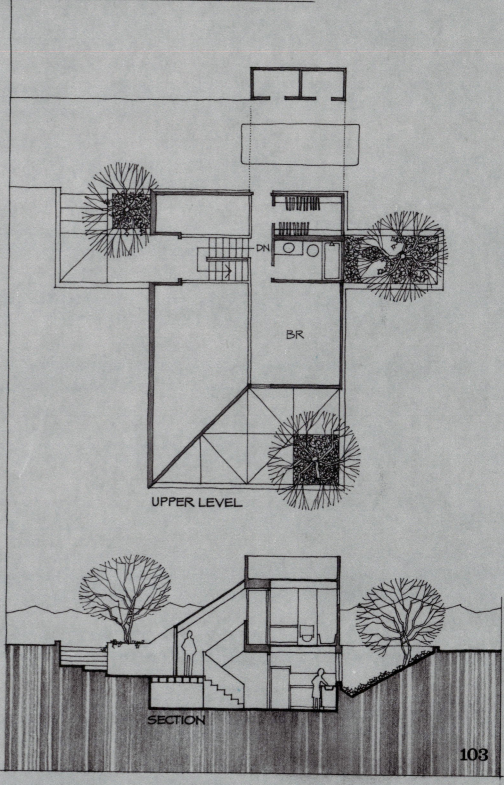

UPPER LEVEL

BR

DN

SECTION

TONAL INTEREST IN PLANS AND SECTIONS
Plans and sections drawn on tracing paper can
easily have tonal interest added by mounting the
tracings on a variety of backgrounds. Drawings on
tracing paper should always exploit the transparency of the medium.

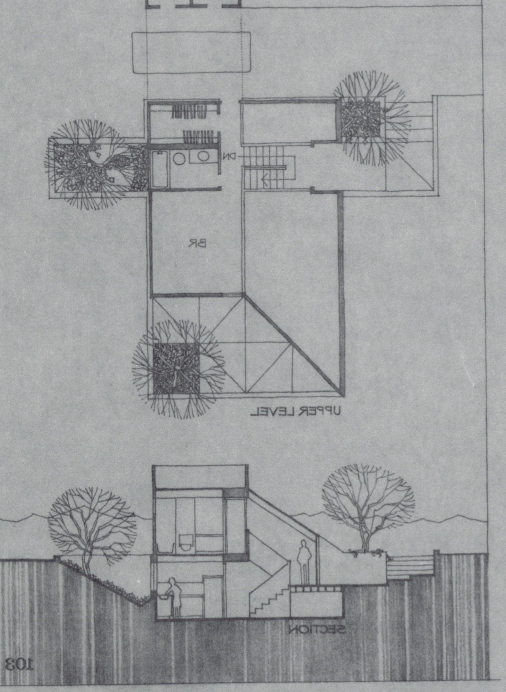

UPPER LEVEL

LOWER LEVEL

SECTION

BR

STUDY

DK RM

K

LR

D

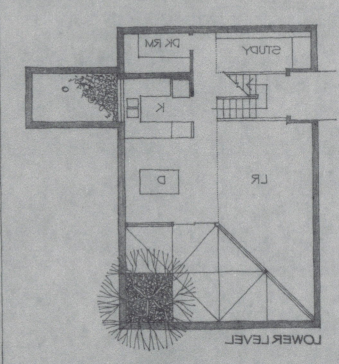

TONAL INTEREST IN PLANS AND SECTIONS
Plans and sections drawn on tracing paper can
easily have tonal interest added by mounting the
tracings on a variety of backgrounds. Drawings on
tracing paper should always exploit the transparency of the medium.

In tracing paper presentations of plans and sections, black backing sheets with a montage of gray and white paper can add the tonal interest category very efficiently. The tonal range should be used, as it is here, to define the various degrees of spatial enclosure.

105

DRAWINGS AS COMMUNICATIONS

I am aware that the initial and most direct use of this book will be as a copy book for certain of the graphic conventions it contains. I hope that some of my lookers will also be readers, and I cannot let you go until I say just a few more things about drawing.

There are signs now of a new interest in design methodology. This interest in methodology is spurred by the demand for sophisticated methods in the race into space, by the obvious advances which more clearly defined goals, more predictable methods, and persistent evaluation have brought to this and other tasks, and by the computer.

My concern is that we realize that drawings have always been, are, and will always be an integral part of any design method architects use. It is time we looked at drawing again, or perhaps for the first time, as a conscious activity, and a communicative language having, like any language, a syntactical structure. It is time we realized that the drawings we use, the order in which we choose to draw them, and our free, creative, confident use of, and continual, deliberate expansion of this language of drawing lie at the very base of any design method.

The criteria for excellence in architectural drawing should not lie in the beautiful or technical perfection of drawing technique but in the understanding and intelligent, habitual and imaginative use an architect makes of drawing as a means of architecture.

The idea that form is as important as substance is as old as Aristotle. This suggests that the form of any communication means as much as its content. Since drawings are visual communications, their form merits careful study by anyone who would use them as communications. Architects communicate as much by the form of their drawings as they do by their content.

The form of communications is usually and correctly determined by the addressee. The difference in form between a love note and a business letter derives from the difference in the person addressed. In categorizing the communication of architectural ideas on the basis of the person addressed, the following categories seem clear:

1. self communication
2. interprofessional communication
3. client communication
4. builder communication
5. public communication

The need to communicate architectural ideas probably began with number four — the construction drawings. This was originally the most critical and still is the most sophisticated in its detail, its symbolic conventions and its degree of abstraction. Cost estimators and building superintendents read a good set of working drawings with great efficiency and clear understanding.

The demand for client communication, perhaps always present, must have intensified with the breaking of traditional styles and the broadening of client options. Unfortunately, this client communication too much centers at the level of style or taste. Architects have unwittingly encouraged this by communicating with clients in a finished, formal way mainly or almost exclusively at this level. The form of the client-communication drawings we use often forces us to the battle of persuasion where we would least like to fight it.

Increasingly complex human activities demanding special environments, the advance of building technology, and the professional teamwork necessary to design large projects on tight time schedules have all made interprofessional communication important. Architects and their professional consultants need to learn efficiently what solutions fellow professionals have found to similar problems. These same design teams need to know how the various systems of a building, for which they are responsible, relate to one another.

The fifth category, communication with the general public, has historically been fulfilled by the building itself. Modern public relations, however, insist on this as one more way to bring the owner to the public attention, especially since the construction of most buildings is a job-producing, economy-boosting endeavor. And so we have the professionally rendered aerial perspective.

Self communication is more important in the design of a build-ing than the other forms of communication, individually or collectively. This creative doodling has surely existed in some form as long as man has taken seriously responsibility for the design of buildings. It is unreasonable to believe that many architectural concepts spring, like Athena, full grown from the mind of even a Zeus of an architect. There is a self-communicative process, and it is not nearly so mysterious as has been believed.

Self communication consists of the drawings which serve as referent models of design ideas. In complex projects these may at first be analytical in nature to help the designer see the pattern of human activity which he is to shelter, or see the physical context in which his building will exist. Later these self-communicative drawings become tentative design solutions held up for comparison with determinants the designer finds in the design task. At some point the tentative design meshes with the framework of design determinants which is inferred by the continual restatement of the problem in the designer's mind. When this congruence occurs, the entire character of communicative drawing changes.

Up to this point the drawings have been entirely honest, open referents, made and examined in all their good and bad qualities. If the designer reaches this point alone, all further drawings become persuasive devices, "commercials," to inform and persuade his professional associates, his client, builder and the general public that his design is the correct, reasonable and beautiful solution to the problem.

The critical communicative drawings are those used to make design decisions. After the purpose of drawing changes from study to persuasion, few honest open choices remain — only compromises when the persuasion fails. The romantic view of the architect or creative person is that he closets his genius and then at some point rushes out with his creation full blown and perfect. All that his associates, his patrons, or the public can do is accept his creation in awe and gratitude or reject his effort as impractical, ugly or unsolicited.

Today's architect cannot operate in this romantic, irresponsible, immoral, stupid way, but the legend persists in our literature, and our schools. Communication and persuasion are not burdens to be borne but an integral part of responsible architectural service and the vital tie with society which architecture should value because of its uniqueness among the arts.

The designer should be able and eager to communicate with his fellow professionals, and his clients at all stages of the design process. We need forms of communication more basic than plan, section and elevation. And it is at this more basic level that the client and our colleagues should participate rather than at the traditional level of finished, detailed architectural drawings. Presented with a slick set of completed drawings, the client, if he wishes to contribute, is left with rejecting the whole scheme or making some inane suggestion like, "Why don't we add shutters?"

The architect should communicate visually with the client very early in the design process. If he would seek and value the client's contributions at this level, it would eliminate the need for "selling" the design to the client at some point. The purpose of drawing then does not change but remains that of making design decisions instead of compromises. This should not become a public relations gimmick, although the client will surely be flattered to be included in what is obviously the formative conceptual level. Presented with abstract diagrams and engaged in discussions of functional pattern, possible meaning of hierarchy and form and their aspirations for the building project, clients can contribute easily and enthusiastically. The idea that an architect's clients are stupid, insensitive patrons to be hoodwinked, however imaginatively, into paying for the construction of buildings beyond their understanding is objectionable on both professional and moral grounds.

This early and continual visual communication will require much additional vocabulary in the language of drawing. It will also demand that the architect lay bare his decision-making process at its most intimate levels. It is on these levels that we should be at our best. Here a creative architect can make intuitive leaps that are impressive and understandable to any client. This communication will also promote an elegant procrastination in the decision-making process concerned with which decisions should be first and let the client and all others involved in the design understand and participate in the development of a hierarchy of decisions.

In order to accomplish this early and continual communication we need to think of the drawings we make in a different way. The profession tends to think of them as being made in discreet phases ending in approval of each phase. The series of drawings tend to be 11111 self-approval, 22222 collaborator and consultant approval, 33333 client approval, 44444 bids accepted. Class 5 may happen at various points in this procession. This way of thinking of the drawings as discreet phases as in a critical path is encouraged by the AIA's description of architectural services as separate activities, punctuated by approvals and paychecks.

This segmented view of the communicative drawings in a design process would be better thought of as overlapping and only generally progressive from 1 to 4; something like 1212123123 123123412341234234234234343434444.

We also need a different form for our drawings and a revision of the previously stated categories of communications. Categories 1, 2 and 3 could be thought of as all one type of drawing. These drawings would be simply *design* drawings and they should look like process, decision-making drawings — vigorous, powerful, direct — including abstract diagrams, charts, cartoons, rough models, perspectives communicating formative process and asking to be changed and developed, never approved or disapproved. For individual clients these drawings should be made on cheap tracing paper, in colorful bold lines and tones, and in great profusion. For more formal presentations to corporate clients they would need to be formalized, taking care to keep their vigor. The idea of process is carried well by the use of overlays actually showing stages in the design development.

We should say with the form of our design drawings, "Here is our decision-making process, we welcome your participation, and we propose to prolong and hold open this decision-making process until you are persuaded that we have reached a level where our professional expertise makes your further participation unnecessary."

Professional delineators, model builders and computer graphics may continue, as they have begun, to take over the categories of communication in the 5, 4 direction. This will only force creative, process communications toward the other end of the scale: toward self-communication and toward more generic forms of design drawing, which can only improve our use of drawing as a means. The computers will no more take over drawing than the typewriters took over writing: the formal documents perhaps, but not the creative scribble.

DRAWING AS A LANGUAGE

A more recent idea than the form-substance insight of Aristotle is the notion of the science of linguistics and the philosopher Ludwig J. J. Wittgenstein that the structure and common use of any language strongly limit and shape whatever ideas come to be expressed in that language. Since drawings, or the series of drawings in a design process, constitute a language, their syntactical structure and their common use limit and shape the buildings built from them in exactly the same way.

Let us assume for this brief discussion that particular drawings can be thought of as the words, the vocabulary, for this language of drawing. We can then assume that their arrangement, the order in which they are drawn, is the syntactical structure of the language. Meaning then will depend, as in a verbal language, on the meanings of the individual drawings or words, modified by and overarched by the meaning of their relative arrangement in the entire design process or statement. Let us call this syntactical statement made by the arrangement of drawings in any design process a *design process sentence*.

In speaking this language of drawing in a design process, architects mumble, handicapped by a very limited vocabulary, plagued by curious speech stoppages and deadly dull sentence structures. To illustrate this in a written language let us write the design sequence sentence of a beginning designer who spends ninety per cent of his time in rectangular plan studies, then extrudes the plan to ten-foot height, plops on a flat roof and in last minute concern applies a sunscreen. The sentence he writes with his design process might be thought of as, "In p–, in pl— pl–plan, in plan—a building should be rectangular, ten feet high and uh, pretty." This is a stammering, dull sentence, written with the design of a dull building.

Now the work of Mies van der Rohe is rectangular and flat roofed but seldom dull. The sentence he writes with his design processes must be more like this. "From a careful, patient, lifelong study of the universal principles of building and the technology of our time, I restate that this building and all buildings should be rectilinear, beautifully proportioned and meticulously detailed."

There is a difference in these two statements. The first is crippled by a limited vocabulary and a dull, passive syntax. Mies' statement grows out of a confident command of the language and dismissal of what he has found to be meaningless words and phrases.

Traditionally we have a meager vocabulary of drawings. This

vocabulary needs to be expanded as does the vocabulary of any language that stays alive. This expansion was discussed under "Other Graphic Means." I have also tried to show how we ignore, misunderstand and misuse the few drawings we have.

Within this vocabulary of drawings, any particular drawing may have several shades of meaning, just as similar words convey completely different meanings. In drawing a space, for instance, a designer may think of and draw shape, texture, light, and color. These are all qualitative, modifying, *meaningful* words in a language.

To say "dining room" is meager and vague compared to "a high, top lit, oval-shaped dining room panelled in oiled walnut." The analogy here between words and drawings is that we can only conceive of those buildings or spaces which we can draw, just as we can only think of the meaning of a certain word if we know the word.

Further we can only think of the shape, height, lighting, texture and color of a space if we habitually draw these qualities in our study drawings. Thus if a designer cannot, and normally would not, draw an octagonal, domed space, lighted laterally through alternate sides, built of rough-hewn black granite

slabs, he probably will never design such a space. So there may be many words which we arbitrarily exclude from any design process sentence we can write because of our limited drawing ability and drawing habits.

We too often arrange the vocabulary we have in the same way regardless of the design question we are answering. Let us assume that a particular design problem can be thought of as asking a question such as, "What kind of a home should be built on a steeply sloping natural site facing a spectacular view?" We can answer such a question with the same stammering sentence as before, "In p– pl– plan— actually in p–plan, in plan view a house should be rectangular, ten feet high and uh, on stilts."

A better answering sentence might be, "On a falling, descending site a home should step randomly, naturally, beautifully down the slope from public to private spaces, penetrated in varying ways by interesting selections of the marvelous view." There are two variables involved in this change. Perhaps the most obvious variable is the addition of qualitative words which expand and make more exact the meaning of the basic sentence:

Home should step down slope.

111

The second variable is not as obvious but actually much more important: the syntactical order of the words, or drawings. You will notice the opening phrase is not "In plan," which forces and limits all that follows according to a particular formal architectural drawing. Instead the second sentence begins with the phrase "On a falling, descending site," which grows out of this particular problem or question and not from some preconceived formal notion.

If we begin all the design process sentences with which we answer design questions with "In plan," or any other such limiting phrase we will hardly be eloquent. Try it. Write a few sentences beginning with such a phrase and you will feel the limitation.

We should rather begin our answering design process sentences with "spatially," or "sequentially," or "in response to the site," or any initial phrase which derives from a carefully developed architectural theory or from the determinants found in the particular design question. Such a sentence will be better than one which opens with a preconceived notion about a particular drawing from a particular preconceived design method.

First we should couch the answering sentence in qualitative phrases and clauses derived from the determinants found in the particular problem and then choose the drawings which will best explore the answer, and especially the order, both in time and importance, of their drawing. For example, the previously restated sentence about the sloping site would clearly call for sections or sectional perspectives as the first drawings.

There is a myth about design method which dies awfully hard. It goes something like this: "The designer should think about everything — all the determinants, plan, section, elevation and perspective, spatial sequence — simultaneously." This is another part of the romance surrounding our profession. Most architects I know, as I, have difficulty remembering seven-digit telephone numbers. We are not mentally handicapped. I think we could match IQ's with any profession. The fact is, however, that thought, like language, is a linear process. It begins, and how it begins, why it begins as it does, and whether this beginning is consciously chosen all profoundly affect where this linear thought-drawing process will end.

Instead of incorrectly assuming that he is thinking about all the determinants, a designer should decide which decisions to make first and which drawings to make first. He should make the first decisions and the first drawings, aware that the drawings are a language and, as a language, they individually and collectively limit and shape any building he designs.

112

DRAWING AS A MEANS TO ARCHITECTURE

This book views drawing as an inseparable part of the design process — not as an end in itself, but as an important means to architecture. This insistence on the relationship between architectural drawing and architecture transcends the usual emphasis on tools and mechanics, concentrating instead on the advantages and limitations drawing offers an architectural designer.

A comprehensive workbook for practicing architects and architectural students, the book clearly describes and demonstrates the various ways architectural projects can be conceived, refined and communicated graphically. Full size drawings and tissue overlays are used to illustrate the use of drawing in the design process, and to explore the relationship of drawing to architectural design.

The author makes a strong case for drawing as an intellectually developed ability rather than a natural gift, and his own well-defined views on the process, use, and technique of drawing lend the book a special authority as a workbook/guide to the development and intelligent use of architectural drawing.

PEPPER PUBLISHING
2901 EAST MABEL STREET   TUCSON, ARIZONA 85716

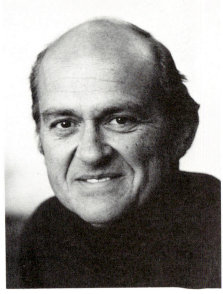

WILLIAM KIRBY LOCKARD

is a professor in the College of Architecture, University of Arizona, and a practicing architect whose work has received awards and been published. He holds a B.S. in Architecture from the University of Illinois and a Master in Architecture from the Massachusetts Institute of Technology.

Professor Lockard teaches advanced design and drawing, and in addition to *Drawing As a Means to Architecture,* first published in 1968, he is the author of the more recent *Design Drawing* and *Design Drawing Experiences,* a complementary text and workbook. This pair of books make the case that the goals, techniques and use of drawing for all environmental designers are so different from ART or DRAFTING that to continue these traditional introductions to drawing is a serious mistake.

ISBN 0-914468-04-9